OD'S END-TIME
BATTLE-PLAN

A BIBLE STUDY ON SPIRITUAL WARFARE

by Gwen Shaw

D1108772

Engeltal Press
P.O. Box 447
Jasper, ARK 72641 U.S.A.
www.engeltalpress.com

INTRODUCTION

There has never been a more strategic hour for spiritual warfare than that which exists right now. We have come to the final winding up of all things. The age which the prophets have desired to look into has arrived, and we are not ready for it. Many of us have had such an easy and uncontested spiritual life that we are untrained in spiritual warfare. I know that God has been speaking to me to help to prepare His people for the final conquest. I believe that most of us will be living to see this final battle. It is important therefore, that you know how to prepare for it so that you might be "more than conqueror through Jesus Christ."

The final battle will touch every life, the young and the old. In a time of national crisis the aged, experienced soldiers are called to take their place in the front lines. There is no retirement for those who are spiritually enabled to stand against the cunning devices of the evil one.

I love the story of Marshal Baron Carl Gustaf Emil Mannerheim, the George Washington of modern Finland. He was born in Finland in 1867. He began his early military training as a lieutenant of cavalry in the Russian army in 1889 and served in the Russo-Japanese war in World War I. By 1917 he was a corps commander with the rank of Lieutenant General. After the Russian Revolution he returned to his native Finland, which had declared its independance from the rest of Russia. He became the commander of the "White Russian" army which fought against the Bolsheviks, and led them into victory in four months' time. He became the Regent of Finland, a position he held for seven months, until a republic was declared.

Mannerheim's finest hour of honour and glory came

when Stalin demanded the surrender of a small, but strategically important, area of the Karelian Isthmus and lease of Hanko peninsula to the U.S.S.R. as a naval base. Backed unanimously by public opinion, the Finnish government and parliament refused to agree to the demands, apart from a minor frontier adjustment. A little over a month after Stalin's demands were made, Russia attacked Finland and set up a Finnish puppet government in Moscow consisting of Communists who had escaped from Finland. It was in this strategic hour of national crisis that Mannerheim, at the age of 72, accepted the command of the armed forces of Finland, although he knew that material preparations for defence had been sadly neglected. The Finns fought heroically and inflicted great losses on the enemy. As a result the U.S.S.R. consented to negotiate a peace settlement with Finland's legal government. But while they were talking peace, the Russians suddenly smashed the Finnish lines on the Karelian Isthmus. Finland could not hold out alone against the superior forces, and finally ceded to the U.S.S.R. the southeastern part of the country, leasing Hanko as a Soviet naval base. The inhabitants of the ceded area chose to leave and settle in what was still Finnish territory. It is a sad story of treachery, but if it had not been for Mannerheim's brilliance and sacrificial dedication in a time of warfare all of his country would have fallen to Russia.

A great soldier uses many different tactics of warfare. For every battle he must use a different battle-plan. Joshua did not always fight the same way. David, who was one of the greatest soldiers, received counsel from the Lord as how to go to battle against his enemy. In II Samuel 5:19 we read, *"And David enquired of the Lord, saying, Shall I go up to the Philistines?"* When God told him what to do, and he obeyed, he won the victory. Later the Philistines attacked him again. Again David inquired of the Lord and this time the Lord said, *"Thou shalt not go up; but fetch a compass behind them, and come upon them over against the mulberry trees. And let it be, when thou hearest the sound of a going in the tops of the mulberry trees, that then thou shalt bestir thyself: for then shall the Lord go out before thee, to smite the host of the Philistines."* (Verse 23) David did as the Lord had commanded him and again he won a great victory.

The battle that faces us is not a small skirmish on the border, but a large-scale, prolonged contest which began in the Garden of Eden and will culminate with the return of Jesus Christ. It will demand our utmost strength, dedication, loyalty and intelligence.

But remember, thank God, that you are not fighting alone. God has given us many weapons of warfare to enable us to win the victory. These weapons are the precious Blood of Jesus, the Word of God, prayer and intercession, fasting, the Holy Spirit and the angelic hosts who are always engaged in warfare against the evil hosts.

The purpose of this book is to help you to understand how you must go to the Lord, like David did, and ask Him what battle-plan you must use in your battle. For every battle there is a different plan, because Satan attacks in different ways. God has many different and ingenious ways of fighting, and He will show you which way you will win the victory the fastest. Why waste your time and energy in a long battle when you can win the victory through the intelligence of the Holy Spirit in a shorter time?

—Gwen R. Shaw

TABLE OF CONTENTS

CHAPTER ONE

WINNING THE BATTLE THROUGH PRAISE

Sometimes it seems to me that the greatest theme of the Bible is praise. Certainly it will play a great part in heaven. Praise has been established as a way of life for the living and for those who have entered their rest in the Lord. We could write many volumes on this subject alone. Our purpose is to stir your heart and cause you to study deeper into these truths yourself. Nevertheless, let us look into the Word of the Lord on this subject for a small but powerful reminder of the power of praise.

Leah

The first one to introduce praise in the Bible is none other than Leah, the despised and rejected wife of Jacob. She knew that she was not loved by her husband. Therefore she sought in every way that is humanly possible to win his affections. She bore him three sons, Reuben, Simeon and Levi; but still her husband took little notice of her, except to perform the duty of a husband unto her. And then she had her fourth son and she named him Judah, which means "praise." She said, *"Now will I praise the Lord."* (Genesis 29:35)

Most of us wait until we win the battle before we begin to praise the Lord. This is good, but it is not enough. Praise must be used as the battle-plan for victory and not as the result of victory. Leah's praises won for her the victory for which she longed. She outlived her sister by many years, and had the honour of having her husband buried at her side. (Genesis 49:31) When you begin to praise the

1

Lord in the midst of your battle, you will begin to lay the groundwork for the victory which you desire.

Praise Opens Gates

In Isaiah we read, *"Violence shall no more be heard in thy land, wasting nor destruction within thy borders; but thou shalt call thy walls Salvation, and thy gates Praise."* (Isaiah 60:18) This glorious promise of victory is given to the people who shall arise and shine in the glory of the Lord in the last days. (Isaiah 60:1,2) In this verse is the key to victory in these days when there is violence in the land and destruction at the borders. The nations need to turn to the Lord, bringing their praises to God like never before. We need to not only praise the Lord, but we need to live a life that is a praise to God and not a shame and disgrace to His holy name.

Are you surrounded by a situation that is impossible for you to escape? Are the doors and windows barred before you? Begin to praise the Lord and you will find that, as you praise the Lord, the doors will open in the wall where there are no doors, and you will be able to come out of your imprisonment and confinement through the "door of praise."

Paul And Silas

When Paul and Silas were in prison they began to praise the Lord, and the impact of their praise was so mighty that it caused a great earthquake which shook the foundations of the prison, and immediately all the doors were opened and everyone's bands were loosed. (Acts 16:25,26) Praise not only opened the prison doors, but it also shook the chains

2

off the arms and legs of the prisoners. You need to praise the Lord so that you can get loosened from your bondages and your bad habits. Praise will deliver you from the demon spirits of alcohol, drugs, nicotine, lust, and every other kind of evil vice that has you bound. Begin to praise the Lord NOW; don't wait until AFTER you are delivered. Use praise as a battle-plan. Praise with sincerity, with conviction and with real faith, for if you don't, then your praise is not a battle-plan, it is a babble-plan. Your empty praise will not reach any higher than the ceiling.

A Life Of Praise

God wants your whole life to be one of praise. The psalmist says in Psalm 34:1, *"His praise shall continually be in my mouth."* Praise is powerful because it glorifies the one we love and serve. Psalm 50:23, *"Whoso offereth praise glorifieth me: and to him that ordereth his conversation aright will I show the salvation of God."* When you get your conversation right before the Lord you will see His salvation; He will save you out of every negative and evil situation of your life. How often should you praise the Lord? Psalm 71:8 says, *"Let my mouth be filled with thy praise and with thy honour all the day."* If we spend our days in praising the Lord we won't have time to talk about things about which we should not speak.

We must learn to live a life of praise. The Psalmist says, *"Seven times a day do I praise thee because of thy righteous judgments."* (Psalm 119:164) Seven is the perfect number. We must praise the Lord whenever we have opportunity.

A People Of Praise

The desire of the Lord is to have a people who shall be a people of praise. This is why He chose Israel. He said to them, *"And the Lord hath avouched thee this day to be his peculiar people, as he hath promised thee, and that thou shouldest keep all his commandments; And to make thee high above all nations which he hath made, in praise, and in name, and in honour; and that thou mayest be an holy people unto the Lord thy God, as he hath spoken."* (Deuteronomy 26:18,19) In these last days He is choosing out a people whom He calls "a people of praise." Unless we learn to praise the Lord and know why we should praise the Lord, we cannot fit into this high and holy calling which He is placing upon our lives. There is no tomorrow; the call is going out today. Even while you are reading this book, God is putting His finger on you and calling you into this company of praisers. Accept this call — obey it, and you shall see His glory; reject it, and you shall know shame and failure.

Audible Praise Blesses God And Defeats Satan

Many say, "Oh, yes, I will praise the Lord, but I will do it silently." That is good, but it is not enough. There are times when the devil and his hosts need to hear your voice. You will make him uncomfortable when you praise the Lord in Satan's presence. Psalm 66:8 says, *"O bless our God, ye people, and make the voice of his praise to be heard."* God wants to hear your voice praising Him and the devil doesn't want to hear it. Who are you going to please, God or the devil?

4

Praise Brings You Into God's Presence

When you praise the Lord, you actually enter into His presence. He commands, *"Enter into his gates with thanksgiving, and into his courts with praise: be thankful unto him and bless his name."* (Psalm 100:4)

When I read this verse, I picture all of Israel coming up to the temple in Jerusalem during the great feast days. They are praising the Lord and worshipping Him and they are making a joyful noise unto the Lord. I can see them rejoicing and exalting Him. Oh, Hallelujah! You may never be able to go up to Jerusalem to celebrate the great feast days in His temple, like they did in the days of old, but you can come into His presence in the same way and He will accept you and honour you and give you His great joy, and you will have revival in your soul.

Praise Accompanies Revival

During the time of Hezekiah's revival he appointed the priests and Levites to give thanks and to praise in the gates of the tents of the Lord. (II Chronicles 31:2) God wants you to praise Him, not only in His house, but also in your tents, your dwelling places. By praising the Lord, you will turn your home into a temple where He will dwell with you. But, on the other hand, it is not enough to only praise the Lord in your home. He also wants you to *"Praise Him in the assembly of the elders."* (Psalm 107:32) Don't be afraid to lift up your voice in praise in the congregation of the people. God has saved us out of heathenism that we might *"give thanks unto thy holy name, and triumph in thy praise."* (Psalm 106:47)

5

Praise God In Front Of The Demons

The psalmist many times says, *"Before the gods will I praise thee."* Why does he want to praise the Lord before the gods? Because the gods are representatives of demon spirits and fallen angels. When we praise the Lord in front of the demon spirits, we are truly engaged in effective warfare, the outcome of which will be victory.

There is a terrible spirit of heaviness over the land these days. This is caused by demonic activity. Satan has come down like a roaring lion, because he knows that his time is short. (I Peter 5:8) He is calling his strongest demons into front-line warfare against the anointed servants of God. When we look at the "army of Philistines" that has surrounded us and hear the raging threats of their Goliath as he roars against us and blasphemes our God, we need to stand, like David did, fearlessly, honouring and praising our God and His greatness in the face of the devil. Perhaps this was the key to David's greatness. He praised the Lord to Goliath. Why don't you look your "goliath" in the face and start praising the Lord! You will be surprised at how accurate your aim will be, and just like Goliath fell, you will see your enemy fall at your feet.

The Garment Of Praise

All the army of Israel was distressed. There wasn't a happy man among them when Goliath defied the armies of the Living God. Saul tried to dress David in his armour, but David knew he had a "garment of praise" which he had received from the Lord in the hills of Judea, as he tended his father's sheep, which would protect him against all the onslaught of Goliath and his powerful, great sword. Hallelujah!

6

David bounded over the hill into the valley with confidence because he was nurtured in praise. When you are nurtured and clothed in the garment of praise, you too will be able to run to face your enemy. Your garment of praise will give you confidence and joy.

The time to wear this garment of praise has now come. God says, *"The Spirit of the Lord God is upon me; because the Lord hath anointed me to preach good tidings unto the meek; he hath sent me to bind up the brokenhearted, to proclaim liberty to the captives, and the opening of the prison to them that are bound; To proclaim the acceptable year of the Lord, and the day of the vengeance of our God; to comfort all that mourn; To appoint unto them that mourn in Zion, to give unto them beauty for ashes, the oil of joy for mourning, the garment of praise for the spirit of heaviness; that they might be called the trees of righteousness, the planting of the Lord, that he might be glorified."* (Isaiah 61:1-3) O, praise the Lord! What a day of glory and victory this is! Put off that garment of mourning and complaining and fault-finding and criticism and self-pity, and put on the garment of praise, and you will be a part of the chosen end-time army which is anointed to preach the good tidings to the meek, heal the brokenhearted, set the captives free, open prison doors, and proclaim the acceptable year of the Lord. You can never give joy to anyone as long as you are wearing the garment of mourning. The garment of mourning, the spirit of heaviness, belongs in the morgue and not in the house of praise and victory. Begin to clothe yourself with praise so that you might be adorned for this glorious ministry.

7

The Sacrifice Of Praise

Jeremiah 17:26 says, *"And they shall come from the cities of Judah, and from the places about Jerusalem, and from the land of Benjamin, and from the plain, and from the mountains, and from the south, bringing burnt offerings and sacrifices, and meat offerings, and incense, and bringing* **sacrifices of praise,** *unto the house of the Lord."*

The writer of Hebrews caught the revelation of this in Hebrews 13:15, *"Let us offer the sacrifice of praise to God continually, that is, the fruit of our lips giving thanks to his name."* God is calling us to continually praise Him. (Psalm 34:1) Sometimes it seems like a sacrifice when you feel discouraged or disappointed or some tragedy has happened in your life. But that is the time when your sacrifice of praise will be the most effective. If you wait until you are happy before you praise the Lord, then it is not a sacrifice of praise. A sacrifice is something that costs you something. Let your lips be the "lamb" that is laid upon the altar in thanksgiving and gratitude, and you will come away rejoicing.

Millenium Praise

The glory of the millenium rule will be that the earth will be full of His praise. (Habakkuk 3:3) If you want kingdom rule in your soul now, then praise the Lord now. You are made of the dust of the earth of this world. Why not fill your own little "world" with millenium praise!

God calls for the whole of His creation to praise Him. *"Let the heaven and earth praise him, the seas, and every thing that moveth therein."* (Psalm 69:34) *"The heavens shall praise thy wonders, O Lord:"* (Psalm 89:5) *"Praise ye the Lord. Praise ye the Lord from the heavens: praise him in the heights. Praise ye him, all his angels: praise ye him, all his hosts. Praise ye him, sun and moon: praise him, all ye stars of light. Praise him, ye heavens of heavens, and ye waters that be above the heavens. Praise the Lord from the earth, ye dragons, and all deeps: Fire, and hail; snow, and vapours; stormy wind fulfilling his word: Mountains, and all hills; fruitful trees, and all cedars: Beasts, and all cattle; creeping things, and flying fowl: Kings of the earth, and all people, princes, and all judges of the earth: Both young men and maidens; old men, and children: Let them praise the name of the Lord:..."* (Psalm 148:1-4;7-13)

Perfected Praise In Children

The most glorious of all praise is that in the life and mouth of the little children and the babies. Jesus said to the Pharisees who were criticising the praising of the children when Jesus came riding into Jerusalem on a donkey, *"Yea, have ye never read, Out of the mouth of babes and sucklings thou hast perfected praise?"* (Matthew 21:16) That is why we must teach the little ones to praise the Lord even from the crib. To see a baby praise the Lord is a beautiful thing.

The Poor Need To Praise The Lord

The poor and needy are exhorted to praise the Lord. *"Let the poor and needy praise thy name."* (Psalm 74:21) When you praise the Lord, God begins to multiply that which you have, and you will be amazed at how He can do it!

When I was about fifteen years old, my father lost

9

everything we had in a business venture that collapsed. We were very poor. In those days people were too proud to ask for welfare. It was considered a disgrace. Winter was coming; our rented house was big and old and draughty. There was hardly any money for food, let alone, fuel. My father and mother had just come into Pentecost after being born and raised Mennonites. One of the things that this new faith brought into their lives was the truth about tithing, so my parents began to tithe. My father, in order to help us survive, got a job as a manager of a farm. His wages were $35.00 a month. It was out of this small and meagre income that he began to tithe. He was worried about how he would support our small family of three children during that on-coming Ontario winter. One day, he went out into the woodshed and he had a praise meeting with the Lord. There was a very small quantity of coal lying there on the ground of the shed. He asked God to be merciful and multiply it. Every day we used coal, and we used plenty of it! Month after month rolled by. Finally, spring came and the weather changed. My father went out into the woodshed again to look at his miracle coal supply. There was as much there as there had been in the fall, and we had been using from it all winter long. God had multiplied it because of two reasons. One: my father had obeyed the laws of tithing to God. Two: my father and mother had praised the Lord every day for the miracle of supply. It was no wonder that later on I was able to live the life of a faith-missionary. I learned a valuable lesson from my parents' life of praise.

Many times during my life of faith on the mission field I have praised the Lord and seen Him come forth in mighty victory. Even now, as the responsibilities of the great missionary ministry of the End-Time Handmaidens continue to grow greater, I continually see the miracle of supply as I praise the Lord. Praise opens the coffers of heaven and pours out to us from God's storehouse. That is why the Lord especially tells the poor and needy to praise the Lord. They need to praise Him even more than the rich.

Scriptural Instances Of Praise

The Bible is full of testimonies of the victories that were won through praise. Let us take time to study some of them. They are important for us to know so that our faith will increase. That which is founded on the Word of God is reliable. It is not enough to praise the Lord because someone tells you to. You must know that it is in the Word of God.

King David

David was the greatest "praiser" in history. Perhaps that is why, in spite of his sins (and they were very great and terrible), the Lord called him, *"a man after mine own heart."* (Acts 13:22) When you praise the Lord, you come very close to the Lord, for the Bible says that the Lord inhabits the praises of His people. (Psalm 22:3) That means that God comes and lives in the heart of the one who praises Him. Don't you want God to live in your heart? Then open your heart to praise Him and worship Him so that you can make a gate in the wall around your heart for Him to come in and live with you.

Daniel

Daniel was facing execution, along with all the other wise men of Babylon. But what did he do? He went to

God alone and sought the Lord for a revelation of His secrets so that the lives of all these great people could be saved. God revealed the forgotten dream of King Nebuchadnezzar, and Daniel praised the Lord and said, *"I thank thee, and praise thee, O thou God of my fathers, who hast given me wisdom and might, and hast made known unto me now what we desired of thee; for thou hast now made known unto us the king's matter."* (Daniel 2:23) Daniel set such a powerful example of praising God to Nebuchadnezzar that, later, when Nebuchadnezzar was delivered of the evil spirit that had changed his nature into that of a wild beast and driven him into the wilderness for seven years, he too, praised the Lord: *"Now I Nebuchadnezzar praise and extol and honour the King of heaven, all whose works are truth, and his ways judgment: and those that walk in pride he is able to abase."* (Daniel 4:37)

Queen Athaliah

The demon-possessed and devil-controlled people hate to hear anyone praise the Lord. When the wicked Queen Athaliah heard the noise of the people running and praising, she came to the temple to see what was going on. The Bible says that when she saw the people standing and praising God in His house she *"rent her clothes and screamed, Treason, Treason."* (II Kings 11:13,14) It is treason to the devil when you praise the Lord, beloved!

Ezra

When the children of Israel came back to Jerusalem after 70 years of captivity they found their city in ruins, the walls broken down, the palaces of the great men destroyed and the temple in rubble. It was a disheartening scene. What did they do? Did they give up, and have a wailing meeting? No! The Word tells us that they rose up to build the foundation of the temple and they did it in a spirit of praise to God "after the ordinance of David king of Israel." It says, *"And all the people shouted with a great shout, when they praised the Lord, because the foundation of the house of the Lord was laid. But many of the priests and Levites and chief of the fathers, who were ancient men, that had seen the first house, when the foundation of this house was laid before their eyes, wept with a loud voice; and many shouted aloud for joy: So that the people could not discern the noise of the shout of joy from the noise of the weeping of the people: for the people shouted with a loud shout, and the noise was heard afar off."* (Ezra 3:10-13)

It was this same shout, when the Holy Ghost fell on the day of Pentecost, that brought the crowd. We have lost our shout of praise. And we have lost it because we do not have praise and gratitude in our hearts. Will we have to go into captivity to be able to appreciate all that the Lord has done for us?

The Angels Praised The Lord

On the night that the Saviour was born in Bethlehem the heavens were full of angels who were praising the Lord with great joy. *"And suddenly there was with the angel a multitude of the heavenly host praising God, and saying, Glory to God in the highest, and on earth peace, good will toward men."* (Luke 2:13,14) The angels set us a pattern of how to praise the heavenly way. Praise should be joyous, happy, spontaneous and glorious. It should not be something that we do because we feel we should or that it is required of us, but because **we want to.**

13

The Shepherds Praised The Lord

The shepherds were not slow in learning the lesson of praising. When they had visited the manger scene they *"returned, glorifying and praising God for all the things that they had heard and seen, as it was told unto them."* (Luke 2:20)

The Disciples Praised The Lord

After the resurrection of the Lord and His ascension we read, *"And they worshipped him, and returned to Jerusalem with great joy: And were continually in the temple, praising and blessing God."* (Luke 24:52,53) Can you imagine them praising the Lord in the dead and formal temple which was under the control of the same men who had crucified the Lord? Sometimes the hardest place to praise the Lord is in our dead and formal churches. A loud "Praise the Lord!" is like the explosion of a bomb!

The Early Church

After the Holy Spirit fell on the day of Pentecost there was tremendous joy in the lives of all the believers. Heaven had come down among them. That is why the Charismatic move never could compare with the early church awakening or the revival that came during the outpouring of the Holy Spirit during the early part of this twentieth century. A real revival is dynamic, life-changing, converting, transforming and glorious, with joy and praises that are uncontrollable. It also brings dedication and sacrificial giving into the life of the one who is revived. The early church was really on fire for God. They sold their possessions and goods and divided

14

them to all that had need. And they continued daily with one accord in the temple, breaking bread from house to house, eating their meat with gladness and singleness of heart, praising God and having favour with all the people. (Acts 2:45-47) Is it any wonder that thousands were saved?! When people praise the Lord it attracts others to them. That is why the praisers are the happy people. No one is attracted to someone who is mournful and unhappy. If you want to be a winner of souls, then get happy. You will attract others to your joy more than you will to your mourning and complaining. Praising the Lord makes you happy and gives you a beautiful, happy spirit.

The Lame Man

Imagine being carried to the temple every day for 40 years, begging day after day for a few more pennies so that you could eat your evening meal! What a pitiful existence! Yet, one day, this man was healed through the word of faith and the power of Jesus Christ in the life of Peter and John. When the miracle of healing came upon his body and he could not only stand, but walk, he went wild. *"And he leaping up stood, and walked, and entered with them into the temple, walking, and leaping, and praising God."* (Acts 3:8) Praising is contagious. When the lame man started praising God, all the people who saw him were filled with amazement. We have all been praising the Lord together with this healed man ever since.

The Heavenly Company

Heaven is going to be filled with a praising company of saints and angels. If you don't like praising the Lord,

15

you will never be comfortable in heaven. John pictures the wedding scene taking place in heaven, and he says, *"A voice came out of the throne, saying, Praise our God, all ye his servants, and ye that fear him, both small and great."* (Revelation 19:5) The entire picture of heaven is one of praises to God. Ten thousand times ten thousand and thousands of thousands will praise the Lord and give Him honour and glory and blessing. (Revelation 5:11-12) The angels will stand around the throne and will worship God, saying, *"Amen: Blessing, and glory, and wisdom, and thanksgiving, and honour, and power and might be unto our God for ever and ever. Amen."* (Revelation 7:11,12) When we praise the Lord we have a little bit of heaven to go to heaven in! We were created to praise the Lord! This is our predestination! *"According as he hath chosen us in him before the foundation of the world, that we should be holy and without blame before him in love: having predestinated us unto the adoption of children by Jesus Christ to himself, according to the good pleasure of his will, to the* **praise of the glory of his grace,** *wherein he hath made us accepted in the beloved."* (Ephesians 1:4-6) Yes, you were predestinated to the praise of the glory of His grace. Why don't you lift up your hands and praise the Lord?

STUDY QUESTIONS

1. Read Daniel 2-4, II Kings 11 and Ezra 3.

2. Memorize Isaiah 61:1-3.

3. Who was the first one to introduce praise in the Bible?

4. What can praise do for us in difficult circumstances?

5. Give an example of what happened when you praised the Lord.

6. What is a sacrifice of praise?

CHAPTER TWO

VICTORY THROUGH SINGING

Music is the language of the soul. It expresses the heart and soul of its composer. If the one who has composed the music is Spirit-filled, the music will carry the anointing for many centuries into the future. I believe that much of the anointed sacred music with which God has gifted this world, will be heard throughout the ages of eternity. I also believe that much of the beautiful music of heaven is yet to be composed or given, through the anointing, to someone who will pay the price to receive it. Not all music is divinely inspired. Some music, even in the recent years, still is tainted by the soul of the one who has not had complete deliverance from the spirits that possessed him in the past. Sad to say, much of this type of music has even entered the church. We have a "mixture" in our sacred music which has grieved the Holy Spirit, but, because the name of Jesus is mentioned in this music, it is supposed to be accepted by the church, in spite of the fact that the one who wrote it has never been completely set free nor delivered of demonic influences which still hang on in his musical career after he was born again.

Satanically Inspired Music

Satan knows the power of music. Remember that he was one of the great musicians of heaven before his fall. Ezekiel, in describing Satan, says, *"Thou hast been in Eden the garden of God;...the workmanship of thy tabrets and of thy pipes was prepared in thee in the day that thou wast created."* (Ezekiel 28:13) The word "tabrets" is the same one used for "tambourine" and it refers to musical instruments that were used in Bible times. This scripture shows us that, as "the anointed cherub that covered," Satan was gifted and anointed for music. When he fell he took this gift with him, for the gifts and the callings of God are without repentance (Romans 11:29); but he perverted his gift, and has inspired his followers with this same perverted "music" with which he is, in these last days, contaminating mortals. That is why you will find that much of the modern blasphemous "music" that is recorded is back-masked (a new word, coined to describe music which when played in reverse has a lascivious, satanically evil wording and connotation) in such a way that Satan is worshipped in this music. Music is one of Satan's greatest weapons to destroy our generation, and he has used it effectively.

It has long been a fact that, even as some music can be so divinely inspired that it will turn a person to God, lift up his soul in worship and draw him into a state of spiritual ecstasy, in the same way satanical music will destroy and bring a curse on all who touch it or have anything to do with it. Such is the story about some of the symphonies which have won fame, or should I say, infamy, through the sinister death and tragedies that have accompanied their rendering. Let me tell you about some of them.

Death Music

The "Pathetique" from Tschaikovsky's Sixth Symphony: If you were to give a recording of it to some musicians, they would turn pale, for they would consider it to be a "gift of death," — either their own, or that of someone close to them. It was a belief shared by noted conductors Walter Damrosch and Arturo Toscanini, who had seen mu-

19

sicians refuse to play or even listen to the Sixth Symphony. Toscanini thought that the tortured soul of Tschaikovsky was imprisoned in the dreadful "Pathetique." Tschaikovsky was Czarist Russia's most famous composer. He died mysteriously in 1893 after conducting an orchestra in the premiere of this symphony. His death has never been explained, nor that of a young nephew and a fellow musician who followed him to the grave.

This cycle of death and tragedies continued to accompany this symphony. One of the most startling was the double death of Maestro Ossip Gabrilowitsch and also a great young clarinist, Ray Schmidt, who died in view of a Detroit audience in 1935. Internationally known conductor Victor Kolar said, "I have played the 'Pathetique' moment 15 times in the past 25 years. Each of those times someone dear to me has died."

Saint-Saen's "Danse Macabre": Like many other conductors and musicians, Toscanini said he would have nothing more to do with this composition. It had brought too many gruesome deaths to the world of the classical music. He had made the decision on a triumphant South American tour with the NBC orchestra. After a brilliant rendition of it, he saw one of his violinists walk into the street, as if in a trance, and die hideously under the wheels of a truck. Hitler himself tried to suppress this feared composition, but without success. When the famous battleship "Graf Spree" was scuttled on the Fuehrer's orders, Captain Hans Langsdorff cut his own throat while listening to a "bootleg" recording of this music.

The opera "Charles VI," by composer Halevy, made its appearance in 1849 with a gala premiere in Paris. But terrified stagehands rang down the curtain when tenor Eugene Masol began to sing the aria, "Oh, God, kill him!" As if on cue, another member of the cast screamed and fell dead. On the second night, at the beginning of the same aria, the wealthy opera patron, Pierre Dupont, died of a stroke. Incredibly, on the third night, orchestra leader Kurt Habenich was the victim of a fatal heart attack. The opera company closed its doors and for nine years the opera was mothballed.

The Emperor Napoleon III insisted it be revived, promising to attend the first performance. An elite audience waited more than an hour for the Emperor to appear. The nervous musicians tuned and re-tuned their instruments. When tension had grown to the breaking point, manager Rene Chartreauz crept like a frightened ghost onto the apron of the stage. He said, "Due to unforeseen circumstances there will be no performance." The audience sat in stunned silence. Enroute to the opera house, the imperial coach had been attacked by anarchists and more than a hundred people were killed in the ensuing panic. Napoleon barely escaped with his life. From behind locked palace gates he issued a single harsh statement: There would be no further performance of the opera in France. Nor in any other country, as it later turned out, has there ever been a performance of "Charles VI." The composer died in poverty, as haunted as the music he had created. (Information taken from *Weekly World News*, February 14, 1984)

I believe that, even as Satan has attached himself to certain music and inspired it so that it brings death to performers and hearers, much of our present-day literature and books have the same taint of evil and corruption upon them which will bring destruction and death to those who touch them. This is also true of some radio and Television programmes. Many of God's own children sit for hours in front of satanically inspired entertainment and allow themselves to partake of the "tree of death" because Satan has already given them an appetite for it. But let us now turn our attention to heavenly, anointed and inspired music.

Holy, Anointed Singers

The Bible is full of music because heaven is full of music. If you do not enjoy inspired music, you will not enjoy heaven. One of the first signs that you are "coming home" will be when you hear the angels singing. And not only will the angels sing but the saints will sing in the mighty choirs of heaven. Oh, how glorious it will be!

As one who has been anointed to "hear in the spirit" the anointed music of heaven, and composed or made it available for others, I feel that I know a little about anointed music. I have never been able to just sit down and "write" a song. Therefore I do not feel as though I am a "composer." I never really composed anything. I only expressed in an audible way that music which my spirit heard. These songs were given to me by the Lord in all different kinds of situations and places. He has given me these songs in boats, on planes, in cars, on my bed, on my knees, sitting at a piano, at church, at home, while working, while playing and sometimes when I am the busiest of all and not even thinking about "writing a song." Suddenly, it is there. I hear it in my soul. Sometimes it is just the melody, sometimes it is just the words, and sometimes it is both. He has given me many songs that I only sang that one time and immediately forgot. Others, I have written out or recorded and therefore have been able to go back and find them again. I thank the Lord for every one of them and never take credit for any. I expect to hear some of the music which the Lord has given me when I get to heaven.

The largest book in the Bible, the Psalms, is really a book of songs. Most of the Psalms were put to music and were sung in the temple during feast days and times of revival. When King David composed his psalms he gave them to the musicians to perform. (I Chronicles 16:7)

Temple Singers

God honoured the temple singers. They were given special privileges. They were especially appointed for their position. They even received their "wage." In Nehemiah 11:23 we read, *"The singers were over the business of the house of God. For it was the king's commandment concerning them, that a certain portion should be for the singers, due for every day." "And all Israel in the days of Zerubbabel, and in the days of Nehemiah, gave the portions of the singers and the porters, every day his portion."* (Nehemiah 12:47) Therefore it is only correct and scriptural that musicians should also receive offerings and "portions" for their ministry.

The singers were also required to live dedicated and sanctified lives, just like the priesthood. *"And the rest of the people, the priests, the Levites, the porters (ushers, and door-keepers), the singers...and all they that had separated themselves from the people of the lands unto the law of God, their wives, their sons, and their daughters, every one having knowledge, and having understanding; they clave to their brethren, their nobles, and entered into a curse, and into an oath, to walk in God's law, which was given by Moses the servant of God, and to observe and do all the commandments of the Lord our Lord, and his judgments and his statutes."* (Nehemiah 10:28,29) Maybe one reason that we do not see the same anointing of the Holy Spirit on some of our present-day musicians is that they have the mistaken idea that they do not need to live as dedicated a life as those in other callings of the ministry; but this is not so. It is time we realize that the calling of the musician is equally great before God and the congregation. Let us give them their due honour, and let them also deserve it by the covenant relationship which they live before us as they walk in God's holy laws. Sanctified lives will produce sanctified music, which will make sanctified saints.

Something that has given me sadness is the way we, today, have a tendency to despise the anointed music of yesterday. Some even think they are "more spiritual" if they never sing from a hymn book. The old hymn-books, which were compiled by the anointed scribes and musicians of yesterday, contain godly music which was written in days of great persecution and suffering and trials. Many of these great hymns of the church will be heard in heaven. If they are good enough for heaven, then who are we to scold them? We may "tire" of them, but if we do, we should put them aside until they are renewed again to us by the Holy Spirit. Some time ago I was going through great trials in my life and it was these great hymns of the church that comforted me more than all our modern songs and short choruses ever could have done. I was sharing the heartbeat of great people like Fanny Crosby, Charles Wesley, Frances Ridley Havergal and many others too numerous to mention.

Who Should Sing?

Thank God, not only are the temple singers encouraged

to sing unto the Lord, but we all have been given a song in our hearts, too. *"Speaking to yourselves in psalms and hymns and spiritual songs, singing and making melody in your heart to the Lord."* (Ephesians 5:19) No one has more right to sing than the "sinner who has been saved by grace." Truly, angels will fold their wings when we sing the song of redemption in heaven!

Let us list some of those who were called to sing unto the Lord:

1. **The righteous:** *"The righteous doth sing and rejoice."* (Proverbs 29:6)

2. **Those who dwell in the dust:** *"Awake and sing, ye that dwell in the dust."* (Isaiah 26:19) You are made of the dust of the earth and you dwell in the dust. The call, therefore, is given to you to arise and sing unto the Lord.

3. **The tongue of the dumb** is called to sing unto the Lord. (Isaiah 35:6)

4. **The barren:** *"Sing, O barren, thou that didst not bear; break forth into singing."* (Isaiah 54:1)

5. **The servants of the Lord:** *"Therefore, thus saith the Lord God,...Behold, my servants shall sing for joy of heart."* (Isaiah 65:13-14)

6. **The daughters of Zion:** *"Sing and rejoice, O daughter of Zion: for, lo, I come, and I will dwell in the midst of thee, saith the Lord."* (Zechariah 2:10)

7. **All who are merry:** *"Is any merry? Let him sing psalms."* (James 5:13)

8. **The redeemed from the Old and New Testament:** *"And they sing the song of Moses the servant of God, and the song of the Lamb."* (Revelation 15:3)

The wonderful thing is that not only are human beings invited to sing, but all of God's creation has been given a song.

The earth: *"The earth shall worship thee, and shall sing unto thee; they shall sing to thy name."* (Psalm 66:4)

The fowls: *"By them shall the fowls of the heaven have their habitation, which sing among the branches."* (Psalm 104:12)

The trees: *"Then shall the trees of the wood sing."* (I Chronicles 16:33)

The valleys: *"...the valleys also are covered over with corn; they shout for joy, they also sing."* (Psalm 65:13)

The first account of music was in the hour of creation when the morning stars sang together and all the sons of God shouted for joy. (Job 38:7) God laid the foundations of this world to the sound of magnificent music. Is there any wonder that there should be a song in our hearts? Don't crush this song which God has given to you.

What Should We Sing?

God has given us a song, a beautiful song. The Word of God describes the theme of our song.

A song of praise to God: *"I will sing of the mercies of the Lord for ever: with my mouth will I make known thy faithfulness to all generations."* (Psalm 89:1) *"I will sing of thy power, yea, I will sing aloud of thy mercy in the morning: for thou hast been my defence and refuge in the day of my trouble. Unto thee, O my strength, will I sing: for God is my defence, and the God of my mercy."* (Psalm 59:16,17) *"I will sing of mercy and judgment: unto thee, O Lord, will I sing."* (Psalm 101:1)

A new song: *"I will sing a new song unto thee, O God."* (Psalm 144:9)

Psalms: *"Sing unto him, sing psalms unto him."* (Psalm 105:2)

26

When Should We Sing?

In the night: *"In the night His song shall be with me."* (Psalm 42:8) *"Where is God my maker, who giveth songs in the night?"* (Job 35:10)

As long as I live: *"I will sing unto the Lord as long as I live. I will sing praise to my God while I have my being."* (Psalm 104:33)

When going into battle: *"The singers went before, the players on instruments followed after; among them were damsels playing with timbrels."* (Psalm 68:25)

In Zion: *"As well the singers as the players on instruments shall be there."* (Psalm 87:7)

How Shall We Sing?

With glory: *"O God, my heart is fixed; I will sing and give praise, even with my glory."* (Psalm 108:1)

In faith: *"Then believed they his words; they sang his praise."* (Psalm 106:12)

In the Spirit: *"I will sing with the Spirit and I will sing with the understanding also."* (I Corinthians 14:15) This is a gift that is given to us when we receive the Baptism of the Holy Spirit. We are able to sing in a language that is unknown to us. This is the language which the Holy Spirit gives us. Someone else may happen to understand it if it is in the language that they speak, but often the interpretation is only known through the operation of the gift of interpretation. To sing in the Spirit gives great victory over the devil and it is very similar to the music of heaven. That is why Satan hates it. It reminds him of the music which he used to hear in heaven before he was cast out. It is not necessary to have the song of the Spirit translated because it is often sung to God and not to the congregation.

With gladness for what God is doing in Israel: *"For thus saith the Lord; Sing with gladness for Jacob, and shout among the chief of the nations; publish ye, praise ye, and say, O Lord, save thy people, the remnant of Israel."* (Jeremiah 31:7) As we sing the song of the exodus of this generation, God will bring His people from the north country, and gather them from the coasts of the earth, and with them the blind and the lame, the woman with child and her that travaileth with child together; a great company shall return thither from the coasts of the earth, and with them the blind and the lame, the woman with child and her that travaileth with child together; a great company shall return thither.

I believe that the time has come for the Soviet Jews to leave the U.S.S.R. It is also time for the Lord's people to come out of Iran, Iraq, and many of the nations of the world. Let us begin to sing the song that will bring them out of these nations. We have fasted, we have prayed, we have travailed and wept, we have born witness of our faith that God will shortly bring it to pass; let us now sing the song of Israel's deliverance! The Word of God says, *"Thou shalt compass me about with songs of deliverance."* (Psalm 32:7)

Where Shall We Sing?

In a strange land: *"They that carried us away captive required of us a song: and they that wasted us required of us mirth, saying, Sing us one of the songs of Zion. How shall we sing the Lord's song in a strange land?"* (Psalm 137:3,4) It seemed impossible for the broken-hearted captives of Judah to sing in their land of captivity, but that

28

is the best time of all to sing. When Paul and Silas sang the praises of God, the prison foundations were shaken. When we sing, miracles happen. If we wait until we come up to Zion before we sing, we may have to wait a long time. Most of the songs that the Lord has given to me He has given in the nations where I have served Him: Hong Kong, Germany, India, Nigeria, Indonesia, Tibet, Egypt, Israel, Taiwan, Canada and the United States. When you begin to sing, heaven comes down and you are not a stranger. Music is a universal language. I have received great blessing from songs which are sung in a language foreign to me. When we were in Russia on one of our trips, we taped the choirs of the believers and compiled one excellent tape from all the nine tapes which we had made.* I do not understand a word of Russian, but I am so blessed by the music that it makes my tears flow. The anointing is on the music. Many have told me that they have been blessed by my music even though they did not understand the words, as I have often sung in English even in lands where English is not understood. Anointed music has the "call of the Holy Spirit" upon it.

In the height of Zion: *"Therefore they shall come and sing in the height of Zion, and shall flow together to the goodness of the Lord, for wheat, and for wine, and for oil, and for the young of the flock and of the herd: and their soul shall be as a watered garden; and they shall not sorrow any more at all."* (Jeremiah 31:12) Music unites us. When you sing you become one with others who sing with you, because music produces harmony which unites us together and helps us to "flow together." If you preach a sermon, I

---

*M3 — tape of Russian Music is available from End-Time Handmaidens

29

may not agree with your doctrine. If I preach, you may not agree with mine, but when we sing together we have harmony and a flowing together in the goodness of the Lord, and this will produce spiritual wheat and wine and oil, new sheep in the flock and the herd, and the people of the Lord shall become like a watered garden and we shall have love and fellowship and will sorrow no more. Much of our sorrow comes because of disharmony. Music unites us and makes us one. Let us sing together in the height of Zion!

Upon our beds: *"Let the saints be joyful in glory: let them sing aloud upon their beds."* (Psalm 149:5) This scripture reveals the humour of the Lord. Can you not see King David lying in his bed and singing unto the Lord with all of his heart? There is no place where you cannot sing unto the Lord.

In the land of Judah: *"In that day shall this song be sung in the land of Judah; We have a strong city; salvation will God appoint for walls and bulwarks."* (Isaiah 26:1) It is always a great joy for me when I make my yearly pilgrimage to Israel and sing in the land of Judah. This is the theme of the end-time song which the Lord wants His people to sing in the land of Judah. *"We have a strong city; God will save our walls."* Hallelujah! God wants His people to go up to Jerusalem with a song of faith, even the song of His promises to them in these last days. If you go up to the land of Judah, and all you do is complain about inflation, inconveniences, rejection and a lot of other things, you might as well stay back in your own country. You can never be a blessing unless you go up with a song in your heart and bless the people with the Lord's song, even His timely song of confidence and faith in His ability to protect and watch over them and fulfil His plan upon them.

On your way to Gethsemane: *"And when they had*

30

sung an hymn, they went out into the mount of Olives."
(Matthew 26:30) After Jesus had finished talking with his
disciples in the Upper Room, he sang a hymn with them,
and then He went out into the night and crossed the Kidron
Valley to climb Mt. Olives where He would pray until they
would come and arrest him. When you face the darkest
hour of your life, whether it be prison, or sickness, or
death, or any other great trial, sing a hymn! It will give you
the strength to face your Gethsemane, to pray alone, to go
with your captors, to carry the cross that awaits you. Never
face the night seasons of your life without a song in your
heart. Try it! It really helps! Most of my songs were given
to me by the Lord during the most difficult times of my
life.

I well remember one night in Hong Kong when I had
been cruelly attacked by a close member of the family. I
silently stepped out on the veranda of my small apartment
on the 15th floor and gazed across the Hong Kong harbour
to escape, for a moment, the cruelty of hate. As I looked
into the night I cried out to the Lord, "Oh God, how long,
how long do I have to go through this?" Suddenly, He
answered me with a song:

> It won't be long until He answers,
> Just pray and wait a little while,
> Though trials seem to last forever,
> He'll help you walk each weary mile.
>
> The clouds of darkness gather o'er me,
> Till all is dark on every side
> But when I cry to Him for vict'ry
> The Lord doth come, with me abides.

Your broken heart just brings you nearer
To Christ the Lord, who dries each tear.
You'll find each heartache makes Him dearer
He'll give new hope, remove each fear.

For many years you've prayed and waited,
Until all hope within has died
Yet God within His Word has stated
His promise holds, He's never lied.

Scriptural Instances Of Victory Through Singing

Moses and Miriam: One of the most triumphant songs of praise in the Bible is the song of praise and deliverance which Moses and Miriam sang after they had crossed the Red Sea and seen the total destruction of the Egyptian army before their very eyes. It was one of the highest moments in victory that has ever been recorded in the annals of history. *"I will sing unto the Lord, for he hath triumphed gloriously: the horse and his rider hath he thrown into the sea. The Lord is my strength and song, and he is become my salvation: he is my God, and I will prepare him an habitation; My father's God, and I will exalt him."* (Exodus 15:1,2)

There is so much more to it and we could write a book on this song alone, but our object is to encourage you to study it and to understand how to write an anointed, spiritual song which will last through the ages. We do not have the original music for it, but some of God's anointed have given us music for some of it and it, too, is a blessing.

Deborah and Barak: Another famous duet in the history of Israel which is recorded in the Bible is the song of Deborah and Barak. *"Praise ye the Lord for the avenging of Israel, when the people willingly offered themselves. Hear, O ye kings; give ear, O ye princes; I, even I, will sing unto the Lord; I will sing praise to the Lord God of Israel."* (Judges 5:2,3)

In this beautiful song is revealed much of the unknown history of the tribes after their entrance into the Promised Land. Some of the greatest secrets of history are revealed under the anointing of the Holy Spirit and the word of revelation through the words of this beautiful song of victory and deliverance which they sang after their great triumph over the powerful army of Sisera.

Israel: One of the sweetest songs of victory is the song of faith sung when Israel was summoned to sing the Word of Faith in the wilderness. They were in the heart of the wilderness. Drought and lack of water was the agony of their lives. One day God spoke and said to Moses, *"Gather the people together, and I will give them water. Then Israel sang this song, Spring up, O well; sing ye unto it: The princes digged the well, the nobles of the people digged it, by the direction of the lawgiver, with their staves..."* (Numbers 21:16-18)

Can you not picture this interesting and humourous scene? The prophets called the princes of Israel to stand there in the desert and dig in the sand with their staves. Naturally speaking, it is impossible to dig deep enough with a stick of wood so that you can find water in the sand. Recently, water has been discovered in the Negev desert and it is many thousands of feet underground. There is no possible way that they could reach this water supply with

33

their staves. But as the people stood around the princes and began to sing the song of faith, "Spring up, O well," a miracle began to happen. The power of God which flowed from the spoken words that were sung out over the desert penetrated the depth of the sandy surface and went down, down, down, far into the earth where a river of water flowed, undiscovered by mortal man. The pressure of miracle-working power began to push at this underground water supply causing it to rise up, up, up towards the surface until at last, under mighty pressure a geyser of water rushed through the sand spraying up into the sky, splashing its flow on the princes and the people who stood the closest to it. They all got soaked! And the water flowed in such a supply that a nation of three million could drink from it and also their cattle. Oh, beloved, have you thought to sing to your hopeless situation? It is time for you to open your mouth and sing over your desert experience. Sing the words of faith, the words of promise, and you will put pressure on a hidden source of supply and God will cause streams to spring forth in your desert and spring up in your valley.

Jehoshaphat's victorious army: One of the most challenging and glorious stories of victory through music and song is that recorded in II Chronicles 20. Jehoshaphat, the king of Judah, was put to one of the greatest tests of faith that has ever been recorded in the Bible when someone came and told him that a great multitude was coming against Jerusalem from the other side of the Jordan. At least three nations, and possibly more, had gathered together to attack God's chosen people. Jehoshaphat knew that they were unprepared to fight such a mighty enemy, so he did the best thing that he could possibly have done; he set his face to seek God and proclaimed a fast throughout all Judah. The people gathered themselves together for the greatest prayer meeting ever recorded in history. The prophet of the Lord stood up in their midst and prophesied to them, *"Thus saith the Lord unto you, Be not afraid nor dismayed by reason of this great multitude; for the battle is not your's but God's....Ye shall not need to fight in this battle: set yourselves, stand ye still, and see the salvation of the Lord with you, O Judah and Jerusalem...."* (II Chronicles 20:15-17)

When the people heard the word of the Lord spoken through His prophet they were so overjoyed that they began to sing and praise the Lord. As they praised, the Lord God gave Jehoshaphat the battle-plan. *"And when he had consulted with the people, he appointed singers unto the Lord, and that should praise the beauty of holiness, as they went out before the army, and to say, Praise the Lord; for his mercy endureth for ever. And when they began to sing and to praise, the Lord set ambushments against the children of Ammon, Moab, and Mount Seir, which were come against Judah; and they were smitten."* (II Chronicles 20:21,22) The victory was complete and they didn't have to lift a hand to fight the enemy; all they did was praise the Lord and sing and sing about His greatness. I wonder what would happen today if a godly nation would fight its battles in this way. Perhaps we may not live to see this happen again in a nation, but if you will stand still and begin to sing and praise the Lord, you will see the same victory in your own life. God will send ambushments. The enemy will destroy himself in front of your very eyes. You will come through, more than a conqueror.

"Sing aloud unto God our strength: make a joyful noise unto the God of Jacob." (Psalm 81:1) As you sing aloud, the vibrations of your song will go out and the mighty angels of God will come and fight your battles for you.

Angels love music. It reminds them of heaven and attracts them to help you. God hears your song. He loves it too. Help will come to you as you sing aloud unto God.

"O come, let us sing unto the Lord: let us make a joyful noise to the rock of our salvation." (Psalm 95:1) As you sing to the ROCK, water will gush out of it to refresh your thirsty soul. You will see the glory of the Lord, for the song of the Lord is accompanied by His glory. Every great revival was accompanied with much singing. If you have a revival in your soul, you will sing and sing and sing.

Music has always played a great part in my life. I can remember times, when I was in far-away mission fields, such as Inner Mongolia, when I would be lonesome and long for the fellowship of my family and loved ones. I would get out my white, 80 bass Hohner accordion which my parents had given me to take to the mission field, and I would sing all the songs I loved in the hymn book. Sometimes the tears would just roll down my cheeks, but it was healing to my soul.

A Miracle Birthday Song

In 1970 I made a trip to East Berlin. It was my first trip to that city and it was a very deeply moving experience. When the dear Christians there heard that I had my birthday that week, they sang a "birthday song" for me. The words were so beautiful that I asked them to please write them out for me. On my way back into West Germany my friend, Sigi, and I translated it into English, but I had forgotten the tune. I tried to write another melody to fit with it, but nothing seemed to be right. Back in Chicago I gave the words to my friend, Dorothy Buss, saying, "Maybe the Lord will give you a melody for these words."

This is exactly what happened! The Lord gave her a

beautiful melody. When I heard it I was amazed, for I realized that it was the same as the original melody which I had heard in East Berlin. God had given that original melody to a German composer many years ago, and then He had again repeated it to His handmaiden in Chicago. It was so unbelievable that I could hardly believe that my memory was correct about the tune. A few years later, when my husband Jim and I went to East Berlin, I asked the Christians there to please sing my "birthday song." Sure enough! It was the same tune. I know that the music for it was inspired by the Holy Spirit. The title of the song is "I'll Always Love You."

Miracle Lyrics

In 1979 when we were busy preparing for our fourth End-Time Handmaidens World Convention, we were working in the office until late in the night. Finally, around 2:00 a.m. I announced that I was going to bed. I left the office and went upstairs, through our living room, to go to our bedroom. But when I looked at the piano and the organ there, I decided to sing for a while before retiring. While playing the piano, some of the staff came up to join me. My husband also came. The Lord suddenly began to give me this majestic melody. I played it again and again. We all admired it and said that we wished we could have words for it.

Then all of a sudden, one of the sisters, Liesel Mueller, sang the first line, Sharon Cooper Buss received the second line, I the third, and Liesel the fourth. A day later, I got the second verse and a day after that Sharon wrote the third verse.

One week later, at the Convention, Fritz Soehlke from Germany was telling us about his experiences behind the Iron Curtain. He told how a young Russian Christian girl had a disease which necessitated her having an operation that included the removal of her voice box. When she was on the operating table, the doctor said to her, "This is the last time you will be able to talk. When you wake up from surgery you will never be able to speak again. Is there anything you would like to say for the last time?"

There, surrounded by doctors and nurses, she began to recite a poem in the Russian language. Brother Soehlke began to read it to us. We nearly fainted when we heard it. It was identical to the words of this song! Brother Soehlke had found it in our chorus book and thought we had translated it from the Russian! He was as amazed as we were when he heard the story of how God had given the three of us, over a period of three days, the identical words to this poem. The song is now used as our End-Time Handmaidens Dedication song. It is called, "We Come To Serve Our Lord And King" and it always leaves a tremendous impact on all who hear it.

Music flows from the heart of God into our hearts and from our hearts to those who hear it. It is wonderful to be the channel of something so beautiful and heavenly as music.

STUDY QUESTIONS

1. Read Exodus 15, Judges 5, Numbers 21 and II Chronicles 20.

2. Memorize Exodus 15:1,2.

3. Why does music have the power to bring life or death?

4. What role did music play in Bible times?

5. Why should we sing in difficult circumstances?

CHAPTER THREE

VICTORY THROUGH THE USE OF
MUSICAL INSTRUMENTS

Musical instruments are mentioned all through the Bible from Genesis to Revelation. They played a very important part in the worship and social life of the people of the Bible.

The First Musician

The first mention of instruments is in Genesis 4:21, where it states that Jubal *"was the father of all such as handle the harp and organ."* Jubal, like Enoch, was the seventh from Adam but he was from the Cain line and Enoch was from the line of Seth. The word "father" is *ab* in Hebrew and it means "father, chief, forefather, patrimony, principal." That means that he was probably the inventor, teacher, musician, etc. of musical instruments. More than one instrument is mentioned, so he must have been gifted musically in many ways. The fact that he was living during the time of Enoch, when there was a real moving of the Spirit of God ("then began men to call upon the name of the Lord") around this time, could indicate that there was a spiritual renaissance even in the line of Cain at that time. This would mean that there could easily have been an awakening of the gifts of the arts, as took place in Italy and western Europe between 1400 and 1600. A renaissance, such as this one which began with the religious awakening through the preaching of great men like Martin Luther, no doubt was responsible for the beautiful and magnificent revival of the arts which followed. If this was true in the middle ages, then it could also have happened in the days of Jubal. Remember, Enoch was a mighty prophet of the Lord, and his prophecies and supernatural experiences with God would have affected all of the then-known world.

The book of Enoch, mentioned in Jude, was lost in almost total obscurity from shortly after the time of the writing of the New Testament until 1773 when the Scottish explorer, James Bruce, discovered it in the part of northern Africa which is now called Ethiopia. Many great, ancient, mystical writings are still hidden in the mountain-caves of the world, such as the one at Qumran where the Dead Sea Scrolls were only recently discovered. The book of Enoch is a tremendously interesting and soul-stirring book which I feel needs to be looked into again as God is preparing to translate a company of people off the earth just like He did Enoch.*

That there could have been relationship and communication between the two family lines is indicated by the fact that Jubal's father's name was Lamech and Enoch's grandson's name was also Lamech. This indicates that there could have been admiration and respect for each other if one was named after the other. Just because Jubal came from Cain's line is no proof that Jubal was an evil person, as some would like to have us think and therefore, every invention of his was evil and so musical instruments are "of the devil."

If you will remember, Jubal's brother, Jabel, was *"the father of such as dwell in tents, and of such as have cattle."* This means he was a shepherd. Do we believe that all people who were shepherds are evil only because Jabel was

---

*"The Book of Enoch" is available from End-Time Handmaidens

41

from the line of Cain? Let us be reasonable. It is not the instrument that is evil, it is what is done with the instrument that is evil. If it is played under the anointing of the Holy Spirit it is a blessing from the Lord, whether it be in the temple or out in the open field, and if it is played under the influence of drugs, lust and greed for money, it is also evil, no matter where it is played.

The name "Jubal" means "stream, river basin, cultural world, hall, sound of trumpet, trumpet player, musician, lyre player." I believe that Jubal must have had a great conservatory of music under his direction.

The instruments of the Bible can be divided into three groups:

1. **Stringed instruments:** The harp or lyre, psaltery, sackbut, lute, gittith.

2. **Instruments of percussion:** The timbrel (a form of tambourine), drum (toph), (of this there were many varieties just like there were varieties of the harp), bells, cymbals, systra (translated as cornets in II Samuel 6:5), the triangle.

3. **Wind instruments:** The syrinx, pandean, pipe or bagpipe (translated "organ" in Genesis 4:21), the horn (in the form of an animal's horn even when made of metal), trumpet (shophar), the straight trumpet, the flute (a pipe perforated with holes, originally made from reeds, but later from wood, bone, horn or ivory. It was chiefly consecrated to joy or pleasure. Then there is another flute mentioned in Daniel 3:7, which was probably a double flageolet, and the dulcimer (mentioned in Daniel 3:5).

The cornet (shofar) was made of the horn of a ram or wild goat or ox. It was of great importance in the life of Israel. I think that some of its uses should be mentioned here:

1. It was used for special signals, such as announcing the year of Jubilee. (Leviticus 25:9)

2. It was used to announce the new year.

3. It was used to muster for war. (Jeremiah 4:5)

4. It was used for giving the alarm by the sentinels on the approach of an enemy. (Ezekiel 33:4)

Two silver trumpets were ordered by Moses, for calling the assembly together, for the signal to march in the wilderness, and for the muster for war and for festivals. (Numbers 10:10)

The flute was used in mourning for its soft, sad tones, and in the temple choirs. They were also made of reeds for the purpose of altar service because of their softer tones.

The name "organ" (*uggab* which means "the blower") is a general term for all musical instruments that are blown. It is supposed to be the same as the Pandean pipe, which was the favourite with the shepherds in ancient times.

The Dulcimer was an Assyrian instrument mentioned in Daniel. It was a triangular instrument strung with 50 brass wires and it was played with two small hammers.

Women Musicians In The Temple

Because music was a special employment of the women, they took a very active form of worship in the temple in connection with worshipping the Lord in music. There no doubt were female choirs. Heman, one of King David's three great administrators of music in the temple worship had seventeen children. Three of them were daughters. *"...And God gave to Heman fourteen sons and three daughters. All these were under the hands of their father for song in the house of the Lord, with cymbals, psalteries, and harps, for the service of the house of God, according to the king's order to Asaph, Jeduthun, and Heman."* (I Chronicles 25:5,6)

Ezra, in numbering those who were returning from captivity, says, *"Besides their servants and their maids, of whom there were seven thousand three hundred thirty and seven: and there were among them two hundred singing men and singing women."* (Ezra 2:65) David mentions the singing women in II Samuel 19:35. In Psalm 68:25 we read how these women-minstrels even went out before the army in time of war.

Skilful Musicians

In Psalm 33:3 we read, *"Sing unto him a new song; play skilfully with a loud noise."* David was an accomplished musician. He also was anointed. He demanded that all musicians should play skilfully to the glory of God.

The School Of The Prophets

The school of the prophets was not only a place of training for giving the prophetic word in the form of preaching, it also was a place where the prophets were trained in music. In fact it was an important branch of the instruction of the prophets. They were also trained and anointed to prophesy while playing musical instruments. This is no wonder, when one realizes that music can be anointed by the Holy Spirit. Therefore, if the music is anointed by the Holy Spirit, it will also bring inspiration to prophesy.

Even today in some churches, some preachers and evangelists preach better with background music. Sometimes I find that music, softly played in the background, is very effective in bringing souls to the altar, for they are under the double impact of the voice and the song, both of which are anointed.

I cannot remember the sermon that was preached the night that I was born again, but I do remember the song that was sung. It was "Almost Persuaded, Jesus Is Calling." I even remember the exact moment I stood up to go to the altar. The fourth line of the third verse, "Angels are lingering near...." That is the moment I stood up and went forward to accept the Lord as my Saviour and to give Him my whole life. And I believe that ever since that day the "angels have been lingering near."

Instances Of Anointed Prophecy With Instruments

Saul's anointing: When Samuel anointed Saul to be king over Israel and prophesied to him that he would meet three men going up to God at Bethel, he said that he would meet a company of prophets coming down from the high place with a psaltery, and a tabret, and a pipe, and a harp, and they would prophesy. It was when Saul met the anointed musician-prophets that something wonderful happened. The Spirit of the Lord came upon him and he too began to prophesy with them and he was turned into another man. (I Samuel 10:6)

Elisha: In II Kings 3 we read how God sent Elisha down to the battlefield to prophesy to King Jehoshaphat and to give to him a warning from the Lord. When King Jehoshaphat asked him for a word from the Lord, Elisha was so distressed at the backslidings of this man, because of his relationship with King Jehoram of Samaria, that it was impossible for him to prophesy. He needed special inspiration from the Lord. He said to the king, *"But now*

45

bring me a minstrel. And it came to pass when the minstrel played, that the hand of the Lord came upon him. And he said, Thus saith the Lord.... " (II Kings 3:15,16) It was only as he heard the music playing that he was able to break through and give the mighty word of God which he gave and which was fulfilled within the next 24 hours.

In the temple: In I Chronicles 25:1 we read about the musicians who prophesied with musical instruments. *"Moreover David and the captains of the host separated to the service of the sons of Asaph, and of Heman, and of Jeduthun, who should prophesy with harps, with psalteries, and with cymbals...."* In verse 3 it says, they *"prophesied with a harp, to give thanks and to praise the Lord."* Wouldn't it be wonderful if we had more of this prophetic ministry in our churches? Why is it that we have less of this kind of demonstration of the working of the gifts of the Spirit now, after Pentecost, than what they had back there in the temple? Could it be that God needs to raise up a "DAVID" in our midst who will lead the people and appoint them into this ministry, training them to prophesy and play skilfully upon musical instruments?

Anointed Playing Of Instruments Drives Out Demon Spirits

When King Saul disobeyed the word of the Lord and the Spirit of the Lord lifted from him, an evil spirit was permitted to come and trouble him. (I Samuel 16:14) At times he became so violent that he was dangerous. His advisors told him to seek out a man who was a skilful player on the harp, *"and it shall come to pass, when the evil spirit from God is upon thee, that he shall play with his hand, and thou shalt be well."* (I Samuel 16:16) Saul felt this was a

46

good idea, so they began to search for such a person. Someone suggested a son of Jesse, the Bethlehemite, saying that he was a skilful player and also a very courageous person and a good soldier. David was sent for and he came from his shepherd's field, bringing an ass laden with bread, a bottle of wine and a kid, a gift from his father. The Word of God says that *"it came to pass, when the evil spirit from God was upon Saul, that David took an harp, and played with his hand: so Saul was refreshed, and was well, and the evil spirit departed from him."* (II Samuel 16:23)

How wonderful that the musical instrument being played in the ears of Saul penetrated his spirit and began to drive out the demon that was tormenting him, and gloriously restored peace and tranquility to his soul!

I know of different ones who have found that anointed music helps to keep peace in the home. Some women have very difficult husbands and children to live with and they have been guided by the Holy Spirit to constantly play anointed music on their tape recorders or record players. The testimonies of many victories over demon spirits are too numerous to ignore.

I believe that God wants His children to become anointed and skilful in playing musical instruments. This generation is not as talented as the one before. Is it because our children waste so many hours in front of the T.V.? Parents do not encourage their children to learn to play an instrument. A few years agó, many children were given piano lessons. Today, about the only instrument that they are interested in playing, is the guitar. I would like to encourage you to seek the Lord about the instrument which He wants to anoint you to play. Everyone should be able to play an instrument just as easily as they can drive a car. It should be the expected thing. It is time to rise up against the powerful end-time demon spirits and do warfare, and if anointed music can be effective, why don't we use this gift which God has given the church?

Musical Instruments Play A Part In Revival

When David went to bring home the ark, he appointed not only singers, but also a great orchestra. They came up to Jerusalem with the *"sound of the cornet, and with trumpets, and with cymbals, making a noise with psalteries and harps."* (I Chronicles 15:28) Oh, what a glorious musical procession that was that day! During times of revival people are anointed to play instruments. I remember hearing testimonies of different ones who were suddenly gifted, during an outpouring of the Holy Spirit, to go to the piano and play it skilfully.

I will never forget the testimony of a young man in Argentina. He was the teen-aged son of a missionary. He was not gifted to play, but he desired that he would be able to play the piano. He had no opportunity to learn, as there were no piano teachers there. There was a piano in the church. He prayed for two months and every day he went to the piano to try to play. He did not know one note from another. And then, one day, the anointing of the Lord's Spirit came into his hands and he struck chord after chord of beautiful harmony. He played and played and played. It was like angel-music. When I came to preach in that church, I heard him play the piano. It was so beautiful and such an unique piano style that I left the apartment of the missionary's home and went into the church to sit down and listen to this young man play. I have had piano lessons as a young girl, and I can play the piano, but his style was so different. When he stopped for a moment and smiled at me,

I asked him, "Who taught you how to play like that? You have such a beautiful touch. You play such unusual chords." He answered me, "The Lord taught me." And then he told me his amazing story which I have already shared with you. This young man has never lost his gift. That was in 1966 and the last I heard he was still playing the piano under the same anointing. The Holy Spirit is an excellent teacher.

We need a revival of musicians in our churches who will play many beautiful instruments for the glory of God.

God's End-Time Trumpeter

I personally believe that Phil Driscoll is the Lord's greatest anointed end-time trumpet player. There may be others, but I don't know about them.

When Phil was just saved a couple of weeks, I was ministering in a church in Florida. He was in the meeting. I had heard about this gifted musician who had been earning tens of thousands of dollars recording for the devil. I began to claim him for the Lord. They told me that he had once played for the Lord. So I bombarded heaven for Phil.

One evening, when I stepped onto the platform to preach, I was told that he was in the audience. I looked around to see if anyone of the orchestra members had a trumpet. When I saw one I asked Phil to come up to the platform and play that trumpet. I didn't know that some of the elders of the church had not approved his playing in the church because they felt there were certain things in his life which he had to get into divine order. Sometimes it is good to be ignorant of the rules and regulations so that the Holy Spirit can lead you!

Rather shyly, Phil took the trumpet and put it to his

lips and began to play, "How great thou art!" The power of
God came down upon him mightily. It was glorious! He
began to shake under the power of the Spirit. When he
finished playing, I said, "Phil, the Holy Ghost is all over
you. You can be filled right now and speak in other tongues."
I laid my hands on him and right there, in front of all the
congregation Phil Driscoll was endued with the power of
Pentecost and spoke in the heavenly language. Oh, what
glory, glory, glory filled him that day! Today he plays over
the great satellite T.V. stations, blessing millions around the
world. When I heard him play by satellite in Australia, the
tears ran down my cheeks and I shouted, "That's my boy!"
Phil and his dear wife Lynn have been a great blessing to
us in many of our End-Time Handmaidens World Conven-
tions. I always say that he is giving Gabriel a little
competition. Wait till they play together in heaven!

Old Testament Revival

In the revival under Josiah in B.C. 634 the skilful
musicians played their instruments. (II Chronicles 34:12)
Every revival is still accompanied by beautiful anointed
singing. Many songs have come out of the Charismatic
awakening.

When the temple, built by Solomon, was dedicated,
there was a great orchestra playing at this magnificent
ceremony. *"It came even to pass, as the trumpeters and
singers were as one, to make one sound to be heard in
praising and thanking the Lord; and when they lifted up*

their voice with the trumpets and cymbals and instruments of musick, and praised the Lord, saying, For he is good; for his mercy endureth for ever: that then the house was filled with a cloud, even the house of the Lord; So that the priests could not stand to minister by reason of the cloud: for the glory of the Lord had filled the house of God." (II Chronicles 5:13,14)

This great visitation of God, even the Shekinah glory cloud that came down from heaven upon the priests heavily that they were slain in the Spirit and not able to stand, was not brought down by preaching or praying, but by praising the Lord with instruments and singing. Oh, what a glorious day that must have been. All of Israel talked about it for days. It was a story that was told and re-told and then recorded in the Bible.

The scripture says that the musicians and the singers were "as one, to make one sound to be heard in praising and thanking the Lord." Brother, sister, we need this same kind of anointed music again. We need it, like we have never needed it before. There have never been more recordings and more choirs and more singing groups than we have now, but we need the kind of anointed musicians that will bring heaven down upon our souls, until we are not able to "stand" in our own self-righteous works any longer, but will be "slain" by the glory of the Lord. I believe it is possible to play an instrument under such an anointing of God that the whole congregation will be slain in the Spirit and be all "as dead men." Hallelujah!

I Chronicles 16:42 calls the musical instruments of the temple the "instruments of God." If they belong to God, then they are hallowed, dedicated and holy things. As such they have every right to be used in the holy place.

We too are called "instruments of righteousness." Paul

says in Romans 6:13, *"Neither yield ye your members as instruments of unrighteousness unto sin: but yield yourselves unto God, as those that are alive from the dead, and your members as instruments of righteousness unto God."* I am "the harp," "the flute," "the trumpet," through which God makes music. Let your life be a beautiful musical instrument for the glory of God. Never allow your "instrument" to become "out of tune" because of sin in your life. Let the Master-tuner tune your instrument for His glory. He can take your old "violin" and make it into an instrument of praise.

'Twas battered and scarred, and the auctioneer
 Thought it scarcely worth his while
To waste much time on the old violin,
 But he held it up with a smile.
"What am I bidden, good folk?" he cried,
 "Who'll start the bidding for me?
"A dollar—a dollar— then two, only two—
 "Two dollars, and who'll make it three?
"Going for three"—but no—
 From the room far back, a gray-haired man
Came forward and picked up the bow,
 Then wiping the dust from the old violin,
And tightening the loosened strings,
 He played a melody pure and sweet
 As a caroling angel sings.

The music ceased, and the auctioneer,
 With a voice that was quiet and low,
Said, "NOW what am I bid for the old violin?"
 And he held it up with the bow.
"A thousand dollars—and who'll make it two?

"Two thousand—and who'll make it three?
"Three thousand once—three thousand twice—
    "And going—and gone," cried he.
The people cheered, but some of them cried,
    "We do not understand.
"What changed its worth?" Quick came the reply,
    "The touch of the Master's hand."

And many a man with life out of tune,
    And battered and scarred with sin,
Is auctioned cheap, to a thoughtless crowd,
    Much like the old violin.
A "mess of pottage"—a glass of wine,
    A game—and he travels on:
He is going once—and going twice—
    He's going—and almost gone!
But the Master comes, and the foolish crowd
    Never can quite understand
The worth of a soul and the change that's wrought
    By the touch of the Master's hand.

—by Myra Brooks

The musicians played a very important part in the temple worship. There were very many of them. I Chronicles 23:5 says, *"Moreover four thousand were porters; and four thousand praised the Lord with the instruments which I made, said David, to praise therewith."*
"And David and all Israel played before God with all their might, and with singing, and with harps, and with psalteries, and with timbrels, and with cymbals, and with trumpets." (I Chronicles 13:8) That is the way to play. Give it all that you have. Put your soul into your music.

53

That is why the blacks are such great musicians. They put their soul into it.

Revival Under Hezekiah

In the great revival under King Hezekiah the musical instruments played an important part again in the worship of the Lord. *"...and the Levites and the priests praised the Lord day by day, singing with loud instruments unto the Lord."* (II Chronicles 30:21)

The majority of the temple instruments were made by King David, or rather by his command. His name was always identified with them, just like we have Bechstein and Steinway pianos, Stradivarius violins, Martin guitars, etc. In the days of Nehemiah, when the children of Israel returned from captivity, it says in Nehemiah 12:36 that they returned *"with the musical instruments of David, the man of God."*

Laying The Foundation And Building The Wall

These instruments were used when the foundation of the temple was laid, as we already mentioned in the last chapter. (Ezra 3:10) They also played these instruments when they observed the dedication of the wall of Jerusalem. It says, *"And at the dedication of the wall of Jerusalem they sought the Levites out of all their places, to bring them to Jerusalem, to keep the dedication with gladness, both with thanksgivings, and with singing, with cymbals, psalteries, and with harps. And the sons of the singers gathered themselves together, both out of the plain country round about Jerusalem, and from the villages of Netophathi;...And the priests and the Levites purified themselves, and purified the people, and the gates, and the wall."* (Nehemiah 12:27,28 and 30)

Beloved, that is revival! The reason our walls are falling down is because we are building them and worshipping the Lord with vessels that are not purified. It is time for the preachers, the evangelists, the Bible teachers, the prophets, choir members and instrumentalists to get their lives purified by the Holy Ghost so that the wall can go up. The enemy is out to get us and we are not prepared. The Spirit of God is calling for the anointed singers and musicians to gather themselves together in a great Holy Ghost repentance meeting where the Spirit can do a work of sanctification in our lives so that we can be protected against the onslaught of the wicked one in these last days.

The Musicians Wore White Robes

"Also the Levites which were the singers, all of them of Asaph, of Heman, of Jeduthun, with their sons and their brethren, being arrayed in white linen, having cymbals and psalteries and harps, stood at the east end of the altar, and with them an hundred and twenty priests [the same number as were filled with the Holy Ghost on the day of Pentecost] *sounding with trumpets."* (II Chronicles 5:12)

The Lord wants us to be clothed in white raiment, which speaks of the purity of the soul. I do not mean that you need to buy a white robe in order to play or sing for the Lord. But I do believe that it speaks of purity of character and holiness of walk.

Those 4,000 musicians must have been beautiful in their white robes that day. I know that Solomon, who himself was clothed "in all his glory" must have ordered the designers to dress these people magnificently. It is not

55

wrong to have a robed choir, and neither does it take from the anointing. Personally, I think it is beautiful. Why should God not be honoured with pomp and ceremony when royalty is? You can come to God's house and worship and sing before Him in your old jeans, but you will honour Him more if you adorn yourself as becometh a "Levite" of the royal choir of the temple.

Welcome Home!

Revelation 5:9, 14:2 and 15:2-3 describes to us the magnificent music in song and instrument which we will have in heaven. People who have had visions of heaven have told about the beautiful instruments there. Dr. Percy Collett, missionary for over 40 years to the Amazon, tells about his visit to heaven and what he saw in the music department. He said the cymbals were 15 feet across. 30-40,000 angels were playing them. The drums were 40 feet across. Jesus was directing the orchestra. When a soul was saved on earth, the bells rang in heaven. The orchestra is all tuned up and ready to play the great bridal procession when Jesus sweeps His Bride through the gates of glory.

In Bible days it was customary to welcome home the war heroes by going out to meet them with music and dance. This is what happened with David when he returned from his battles with the Philistines. *"And it came to pass as they came, when David was returned from the slaughter of the Philistine, that the women came out of all cities of Israel, singing and dancing, to meet king Saul, with tabrets, with joy, and with instruments of musick. And the women answered one another as they played, and said, Saul hath slain his thousands, and David his ten thousands."* (I Samuel 18:6,7)

When we come home, battle-worn and battle-scarred, the first thing we will hear, will be the daughters of Zion coming out to meet us, singing and dancing and rejoicing. Oh, what a day that will be! The glory will be so great, that we will hardly be able to stand it. And that day is coming soon. It is coming very, very soon. Let us prepare our hearts, sanctify our lives and be ready. It could happen before you finish reading this book!

Musical Instruments Mentioned In The Bible

A large number of different musical instruments were mentioned in the Bible. Some of them have been lost in antiquity. I would like to give you a brief list of references to some of them.

The trumpet: I Chronicles 13:8, I Chronicles 16:42; II Chronicles 7:6; Psalm 98:6; Psalm 150:3; Hosea 5:8.

The trumpet used for war: Numbers 10:8,9; Numbers 31:6,7; Joshua 6:4; Judges 3:27; Judges 6:34; I Samuel 13:3; II Samuel 2:27,28; II Samuel 20:1; II Chronicles 13:12; Job 39:24; Ezekiel 33:3.

The trumpet used in worship: Leviticus 25:9,10; Numbers 10:10; I Kings 1:34; II Kings 9:13; II Kings 11:14; II Chronicles 5:12; II Chronicles 20:28; II Chronicles 29:26; Ezra 3:10, Nehemiah 12:35; Isaiah 27:13.

The psaltery: I Samuel 10:5; II Samuel 6:5; I Kings 10:12; I Chronicles 13:8; 15:16; II Chronicles 5:12; II Chronicles 9:11; II Chronicles 29:25; Nehemiah 12:27; Psalm 33:2; Psalm 81:2; Psalm 150:3; Daniel 3:5.

The tabret: Genesis 31:27; I Samuel 10:5; I Samuel 18:6; II Samuel 6:5; Isaiah 5:12; Isaiah 24:8; Ezekiel 28:13.

The pipe: Genesis 4:21; I Samuel 10:5; Job 21:12; Job 30:31; Isaiah 5:12; Ezekiel 28:13.

The harp: Genesis 4:21; Genesis 31:27; I Samuel 10:5; I Samuel 16:23; II Samuel 6:5; I Kings 10:12; I Chronicles 13:8; I Chronicles 15:16; I Chronicles 25:3; II Chronicles 5:12; II Chronicles 9:11; II Chronicles 29:25; Nehemiah 12:27; Job 21:12; Psalm 33:2; Psalm 81:2; Psalm 137:2; Psalm 150:3; Isaiah 5:12; Isaiah 24:8; Daniel 3:5; Revelation 5:8; Revelation 14:2; Revelation 15:2.

The cornet: II Samuel 6:5; Psalm 98:6; Daniel 3:5; Hosea 5:8.

The cymbals: II Samuel 6:5; I Chronicles 13:8; I Chronicles 15:16; I Chronicles 16:42; II Chronicles 5:12; II Chronicles 29:25; Ezra 3:10; Nehemiah 12:27; Psalm 81:2; Psalm 150:4.

The timbrel: Exodus 15:20; Judges 11:34; II Samuel 6:5; I Chronicles 13:8; Job 21:12; Psalm 68:25; Psalm 81:2; Psalm 150:5.

The organ: Genesis 4:21; Job 21:12; Job 30:31; Psalm 150:4.

The instrument of 10 strings: Psalm 33:2.

The dulcimer: Daniel 3:5.

The flute: Daniel 3:5.

The viol: Isaiah 5:12; Isaiah 14:11; Amos 5:23.

The sackbut: Daniel 3:5.

The full orchestra: II Samuel 6:15; I Chronicles 23:5; II Chronicles 15:12-14; II Chronicles 29:27; Ezra 3:10; Nehemiah 12:27; Psalm 68:25; Daniel 3:5.

The musicians: Genesis 4:21; I Samuel 16:16; I Samuel 18:10; II Kings 3:15; I Chronicles 25:7; II Chronicles 34:12; Psalm 28:7.

STUDY QUESTIONS

1. Read II Chronicles 30 & 34, Ezra 3.

2. Memorize Romans 6:13.

3. Where are musical instruments first used in the Bible?

4. How are music and prophecy connected in the Scriptures?

5. Describe from your own experience how music has brought you into a deeper relationship with God.

6. In what way are we instruments?

CHAPTER FOUR

VICTORY THROUGH DANCING

The word "dance" in the scriptures is taken from several different Hebrew and Greek words.

1. *Chiyl* (kheel), which means "to twist or whirl in a circular or spiral manner, to dance, to bring forth, to calve, to drive away, to shake, to travail." (Judges 21:21)

2. *Raqad* (raw-kad), which means "to stamp, to spring about (wildly or for joy), dance, jump, leap, skip." (Job 21:11) This describes the dancing of children.

3. *Machowl* (maw-khole), which means "to dance, a round." (Psalm 149:3, Psalm 150:4)

4. *Karar* (kaw-rar), which means "to dance, whirl." (II Samuel 6:14 uses this word to describe King David dancing.)

In The New Testament

1. *Orcheomai* (or-kheh-om-ahee), which is taken from a word meaning "a row or ring; to dance (from the rank-like or regular motion)."

2. *Choros* (khor-os), which means "a ring, a round-dance, dancing." (Used in Luke 15:25 when the prodigal son came home).

There are a few others, but this will suffice to let us understand that when the scriptures speak about dancing, it means to literally "dance."

When Is Dancing Wrong?

There is no doubt that Satan has a counterfeit for everything that is good. He is not the originator of anything.

60

He only takes the good thing and he perverts it. Dancing is not evil just because Satan has promoted it. But we must understand also how Satan has used this expression of joy and praise and worship in an evil way.

1. **Before the golden calf (Exodus 32:19):** When Moses was coming down from the mountain where he had received the tablets whereon God had graven the Ten Commandments, he heard the sound of shouting and then he realized that it was the noise of "them that sing." The Word of God says, *"And it came to pass, as soon as he came nigh unto the camp, that he saw the calf, and the dancing: and Moses' anger waxed hot, and he cast the tables out of his hands, and brake them beneath the mount."*

When the children of Israel had made their golden calf and begun to worship it, they worshipped with the dance of Egypt. There was madness in this dance because they became demon-possessed or demon-controlled when they danced before the idol which they had made. This is proven by the fact that they stripped themselves naked. *"And when Moses saw that the people were naked; (for Aaron had made them naked unto their shame among their enemies:)."* (Exodus 32:25)

This kind of stripping and dancing is still very popular in the world today. There is no doubt that when Solome, Herodias' daughter danced before her stepfather, Herod, she performed this type of a dance. Heathenistic dancing was accompanied with scenes of debauchery.

2. **The sensual dance (Matthew 14:6, Mark 6:22):** The second kind of evil dancing was that done by Salome, which we already mentioned. It enchanted and aroused the king (her own stepfather) in such a way that he did a foolish and unwise thing when he promised her that she could have

anything she wanted, even unto half of his kingdom.

The Sacred Dance

Sacred dancing was usually done by the women alone or the men alone. One leads off in the dance and the others follow in the exact imitation of the varied movements that the leader makes. They are entirely extemporaneous, governed by no fixed rule, but varied according to the pleasure of the leader. Dancing was usually performed in the daytime and in open air. It was an outward expression of great joy.

It is wrong to suppose, as some do, that the dancing was limited to the women. When I am in Jerusalem I always see more Jewish men than women dancing at "The Wall" during days of celebration and Bible feast days. It is perfectly scriptural for the men to dance before the Lord and to rejoice.

Scriptures on Dancing

Ecclesiastes 3:4, "... a time to dance." I believe that the time has now come for the church to accept the truth of the victory which comes through dancing the dance of victory and praise and worship before the Lord. In Ecclesiastes 3:4 it says, there is "... a time to mourn, and a time to dance." The mourning comes first. You need to enter into the ministry of travail and intercession and fasting and weeping and only then will you qualify to dance and rejoice before the Lord. Many try to enter into the dance of victory before the "son has been born." First MUST come the travail. If you try to avoid God's Bible pattern, you will come into error and confusion. I have written a Bible study on fasting, called *Your Appointment With God,* and another on travailing intercessory prayer, called *Pour Out Your Heart.** It is important that you study what the Word of God has to say about these truths before you move into the realm of dancing in the Spirit.

To you who have mourned and wept and fasted God is saying, "Move on into praising and dancing and worshipping Him with the **song of deliverance.**"

Psalm 30:11, *"Thou hast turned for me my mourning into dancing; thou hast put off my sackcloth, and girded me with gladness."* I believe that the Lord wants to turn your mourning into dancing. He wants you to take off your "sackcloth" and put on your "dancing shoes" and begin to rejoice before the Lord with great joy and gladness. You have wept and you have suffered and you have paid the price of "going forth and weeping, bearing your precious seed" and now the time has come for you to return, "rejoicing and bringing your sheaves with you." Hallelujah!

Psalm 149:2,3, *"Let Israel rejoice in him that made him: let the children of Zion be joyful in their King. Let them praise his name in the dance: let them sing praises unto him with the timbrel and harp."*

It gives the Lord great joy when He sees His children rejoicing with Him in dancing and praising.

Jeremiah 31:13, *"Then shall the virgin rejoice in the dance, both young men and old together: for I will turn their mourning into joy, and will comfort them, and make them rejoice from their sorrow."*

---

*The two books "Your Appointment With God" and "Pour Out Your Heart" by Gwen Shaw are available from End-Time Handmaidens

The promise of final victory includes the joyful dancing of the redeemed. It says here very clearly that not only women would dance the dance of victory and deliverance, but young men and old men would also join this dance.

Jeremiah 31:4, *"Again I will build thee, and thou shalt be built, O virgin of Israel: thou shalt again be adorned with thy tabrets* [tambourines], *and shalt go forth in the dances of them that make merry."*

I believe that we grieve the Lord when we refuse to express our joy and appreciation in the dance. Don't let your stubborn rebellion reach into your feet.

Examples Of Dancing In The Bible

1. **The daughters of Shiloh:** Judges 21:21,23, *"And see, and behold, if the daughters of Shiloh come out to dance in dances, then come ye out of the vineyards, and catch you every man his wife of the daughters of Shiloh, and go to the land of Benjamin...And the children of Benjamin did so, and took them wives...."*

Perhaps the reason that there are so many "unwanted maidens" is because they have never danced the victory-faith dance for God to give them husbands!! What man desires a sad-looking woman? It is the joy and the beauty which she expresses in the dance that attracts him to her. Seriously speaking, however, it is as we dance before the Lord, our heavenly Bridegroom, that we win His approval and admiration and He, too, will give us the desire of our heart...even unto more than half of His Kingdom. Hallelujah! Surely he can outdo old King Herod!

2. **Miriam and the women of Israel:** Exodus 15:20, *"And Miriam the prophetess, the sister of Aaron, took a timbrel in her hand; and all the women went out after her*

with timbrels and with dances."

Miriam was over 80 years of age. She probably was even older than 90. Yet, after all these years of slavery, God had put a spring in her feet and filled her whole body with the joy of deliverance, and all she could do was to begin to lead these women in the dance of victory. She couldn't stand still any longer, and they all followed her. Can you imagine thousands of women on the shore of the Red Sea dancing before the Lord! It must have been a glorious sight to behold.

It says here that she was "the prophetess." If anyone has a right to dance before the Lord it is those who are called into prophetic ministry. I believe that there must have been many times before their deliverance out of Egypt that she prophesied about that day of victory. And now she saw it happen with her own eyes. She was so old, and many times she must have almost given up the hope of ever seeing her prophecy fulfilled. But God did not let her die before she saw the Lord's glory and might. I believe that many now living will dance the great dance of victory as they see what great things the Lord has done for them in allowing them to see all the scripture and promises fulfilled concerning the consummation of this age.

3. Dancing after victory in battle: I Samuel 18:6,7, *"And it came to pass as they came, when David was returned from the slaughter of the Philistine, that the women came out of all cities of Israel; singing and dancing, to meet king Saul, with tabrets, with joy, and with instruments of musick. And the women answered one another, as they played, and said, Saul hath slain his thousands, and David his ten thousands."*

That was the greatest "street dance" in history! I remember after World War II, when we had won the victory,

65

how the people rejoiced in Canada. Our little town was filled with happy people. The whistles blew, the car horns tooted, the flags flew and the main street was closed off to traffic. The town orchestra came out in their Sunday-best uniform and all of the girls wore their prettiest dresses. The whole town was there to dance and rejoice. Of course there were those who wept too because their husbands and sons would not come home. They were among the fallen who had given their lives that we might have the victory. But what a time of rejoicing it was! Think of what it will be like when the last battle has been won and the last martyr has given his life for the Lord! No wonder heaven will be full of rejoicing people!

Dr. Percy Collett who spent 5½ days in heaven tells us that the sea of glass is the "dance floor" of heaven. He said it is 1,500 miles square and that God's people are always dancing and praising the Lord on this great heavenly dance floor. He even danced with Smith Wigglesworth and his own dear old mother on that heavenly dancing floor.

Heaven is not going to be a dull place. It is going to be full of joy and victory and praise. But how can you praise the Lord without dancing and rejoicing in music, the song and the dance? Have you ever noticed how trouble-making people seldom dance the dance of the Lord?

4. The prodigal son's welcome-home dance: (Luke 15:11-24) This is the beautiful story of pardon and forgiveness. There was a great welcome-home feast. The father ordered the fatted calf to be killed and a great round of festivities to begin. There was music and dancing. Joy filled the father's heart. If dancing displeased the Lord, then Jesus would never have put dancing into the story of the prodigal son. Let us be careful that we don't go beyond the scriptures in our rigid and traditional beliefs.

66

The only one who resented the dancing and rejoicing was the elder brother who was filled with bitterness and resentment. He is a picture of the moral, hard-working, dutiful and reliable Christian elder brother. We see him sulking outside and refusing to come into the house of the father. Many today who think they are perfect before God because they have been so faithful with their works and their donations to God are going to miss out in the end as they see the Lord pouring out His Spirit on the publicans and harlots, the divorcees and the former drug-addicts. And they will wonder how God could send revival and not send it to them when they are so "holy." So they will say, "It is not of God. If it was of God, we would have been the first to have received the revival." Let us be careful that our critical spirit does not keep us out of the end-time victory dance!

5. **King David dancing as he brings the ark of the Lord to Jerusalem:** (II Samuel 6:1-23; I Chronicles 15:1-29) David had tried once to bring the ark back to Jerusalem, but a terrible tragedy happened because he didn't do it the Bible way. He left the ark in the house of Obededom. Obededom means "the servant of the servants." God blessed the house of Obededom in a mighty way.

I hear a good report. "God is blessing the servants and the love slaves." God is blessing the women who are God's handmaidens. God is blessing the men who are God's servants. God is not blessing in the beautiful temples and cathedrals, but in the little cottage prayer meetings and halls all around the world. The Spirit of God is moving all over the world. And the day that we put our "hand" on this move of God to stop it, is the day that there will be "death in our camp."

David had heard the report of how God was blessing

the house of Obededom and a new hope and faith came into his heart. He said, "Do you suppose that it is not a hopeless case, and that we could get the ark back home after all?"

He had prepared a little tabernacle and for three months the tabernacle had stood there and every time he looked at it, it mocked him and the devil laughed at him and said, "Ha, ha, you thought you would bring back the glory of God."

Have you ever had the devil mock you after you have put your heart into a thing and poured out your life to fulfil a vision which God has given you? You have felt the burden of the Lord and you were sure that God had spoken to you and you knew in your spirit that God was going to do a new thing and you sacrificed for it, and when you had done all you could, it all fell to pieces? And the devil mocks you and ridicules you, and tries to kill your faith in God and yourself. He mocks you and says, "Who do you think you are? How can God use you? Look at the mess you are in. If you were perfect, maybe God could use you, but never will He use you now."

If you are willing to wait and pray and find the battle-plan, there will be an answer to your problem. There isn't a problem too big for God to solve.

There is a Bible pattern. When David searched the scriptures and found the Bible pattern for bringing back the ark, he had an open heaven. God said to Moses, *"...See... that thou make all things according to the pattern shewed to thee in the mount."* (Hebrews 8:5)

God had told Moses on the mount that the ark was to be carried on the shoulders of the Levites, men who were ordained by God for the task. God had anointed Moses and Moses had anointed them. Everyone who served in the tabernacle had been anointed with the blood and the oil. It was on their heads, their thumbs and their toes. That anointing was an impartation directly from the glory of God on Mt. Sinai, by way of Moses. And they had to have that impartation before they were qualified to bring the glory of the Lord into Jerusalem.

You can have a thousand hands laid on you by a thousand "Moseses" but unless your "Moses" has received the anointing from the glory of God on the mount of glory, it will all be emptiness.

David went one more time in humility, but with great gladness, to bring home the ark because he had heard from God. I believe that when it says, "he went with gladness" that he had received a message of confidence from God that gave him new faith and courage to try one more time and he knew that this time he would succeed. If something goes wrong, it is necessary for you to take spiritual inventory and find out why and where it went wrong. Maybe you missed God somewhere.

"And it was so, that when they that bare the ark of the Lord had gone six paces, he sacrificed oxen and fatlings." (II Samuel 6:13)

Six is the number of "man." They went as far as man can go in their own strength. And then they stopped and made a sacrifice of the fatlings.

God is calling you to a sacrifice of the "fatlings." He is even calling you to a fast. You have been going those "six paces" for most of your life and now God says, "sacrifice the fat in a good Holy Ghost anointed fast!" God wants to use you to bring home the ark and unless you get the "fatlings" all offered up with a good, Holy Ghost anointed fast, you won't complete the rest of your journey. It was after they made the sacrifice of the fatlings that the anointing came down and they could dance. Those who fast, have a right to dance. Some of you have lost your anointing to dance because it is time for another fast in your life. Those who have been set free from bondages and burdens have a right to dance. Those who have tried and failed and become discouraged, have given up, and then heard the word of the Lord, "Try one more time," have a right to dance. Glory to God!

David began to dance before the Lord. He didn't just do a little skip and a hop! The Bible says, he danced with all his might. Some of you reading this, need to enter into the dance of joy and victory. God says, "I want to set you free!" But you say, "I am too reserved. I come from a conservative church. In our organization we don't believe in dancing. We believe that everything should be done decently and in order in the house of the Lord."

Well, then I am afraid that you will never feel "at home" in heaven. You just better find yourself another future. Heaven is going to be full of dancing and singing and praising and shouting. Glory to God!

I want to be a part of that dancing company that dances its way out of Egypt. If you want to stay in Egypt and sit behind those "fleshpots of slavery," you can stay there, but I am going down to the house of Obededom and I am going to bring the ark of the Lord back to Jerusalem with dancing and praising and shouts of victory. I want to see the glory of the Lord.

On this state occasion, David was no doubt wearing his royal crown and the finest new robe that his servants could make for him. It was probably of beautiful brocade with gold and silver embroidery. But it was only an encumberance to him. David never did like a lot of "fancy dress." He had refused Saul's armour too. And that day he stripped himself of that royal robe and he was wearing his ephod, a simple priestly garment. It is time for us to get rid of the traditional robes of ecclesiasticism which only encumber our dance. It is time to stand in the simplicity of a sanctified, holy, priestly robe, and the anointing of God will come on us and we won't be able to stop our feet from dancing.

And, oh how the people shouted! The trumpets blew all the way to Jerusalem. It was a long journey that they made. He danced all the way. It wasn't just a ten-minute dance. He danced for hours.

As he was coming into the city, there was "an eye" watching him. And every church has that "critical eye." It was the daughter of the former king, even King Saul. She is a type of the traditional Pharisees and hypocrites, those who have been trained in the protocol of dead tradition — those who are programmed. There she stood, looking out of the royal palace window. "Tch! Tch! Isn't it a shame. Look at him! It's unbelievable! Where is that beautiful robe that he was wearing when he left the palace this morning? Where in the world did he put it? And where is his gown? Look at him in his underwear! He is making a disgrace of himself. I'm embarrassed. My father would never have done a thing like that!"

No! He wouldn't have. But he lost his crown too.

You may say, "I don't want to dance." I warn you, watch out, or you may lose your crown. You better move out in the dance when the Spirit is moving. Get yourself up off your seat and let the Holy Ghost refresh you in the dance. Remember, He says, "Praise his name in the dance."

In Psalm 149, the wonderful Psalm on dancing and praising, it says that dancing will *"bind their kings with chains, and their nobles with fetters of iron; To execute upon them the judgment written: this honour have all his*

71

saints." (Psalm 149:8,9)

When you dance, you bind "the kings" with chains. Those demon-kings, those principalities and powers and rulers of darkness, those princes of hell are bound by your dancing the joyful dance of victory. When you dance before the Lord, you are binding the works of the devil just as sure as you do when you rebuke him and when you cast him out. You can even dance the devil out. They do that in Africa. The Christians will take the demon-possessed, put him in the centre, and then they begin to praise the Lord and dance around him, shouting and singing, and it is not long before the demons come out of that person and he is delivered, set free and healed. It happens all the time. It is time we learn about real battle-plans from the dark places of the world where the biggest battles rage and where the devil's power is the greatest. If you want God to bless you...start dancing.

When David had brought the ark of the Lord and set it in its place in the tabernacle which he had made for it, he offered burnt offerings and peace offerings unto the Lord. And then he blessed the people. But that was not all! He *"dealt among all the people, even among the whole multitude of Israel, as well to the women as men, to every one a cake of bread, and a good piece of flesh, and a flagon of wine."* (II Samuel 6:19)

Wine: He had enough for the vast multitude. He gave them bread and flesh and wine. And that wasn't grape juice! Some of us need more of the Holy Ghost joy of the Lord in our lives. We need the heavenly wine in our souls. We need to be "drunk in the Spirit." The power of God can do it to you. In the olden days people got so "drunk in the Spirit" that they couldn't walk home from the meetings. People had to carry them home. It's time for that kind of a visitation again. When you dance before the Lord, you get released in the Spirit and you get an anointing that enables you to share the wine of joy.

That wine made them happy. It made them forget their trouble. It made them forget their burdens. It made them rejoice. They started loving each other. Some of you can only begin to love each other when you drink the Holy Ghost "wine."

Bread: Bread speaks of the Word of God. Some wonder why they haven't got a fresh word from God. They read all of the commentaries and when they get up to speak, they sound like a "dead dictionary." Until you start dancing, you haven't got anything to give your people. When David danced before the Lord, he had the bread. The young people of this generation call money "bread" and you can say that this is typical too of what God will do for you when you dance before the Lord. Finances will be released and money will come into your treasury. I have seen more money come in when we danced before the Lord than when we cried and prayed for it.

Meat: That is a type of strong revelation, even the Rhema of God. It is something that you can "sink your teeth into." It's a good, old-fashioned Holy Ghost "T-bone steak." God gives us something more than the food of babes. God gives us meat for the inner man that satisfies our inner soul.

We have danced our way to Jerusalem and the King has given us bread, meat and wine. Open your heart. Ask God to pour in the wine. Cry out, "Lord, give me your joy. Give me your victory. Give me your glory. Give me your blessing. I want to be drunk in the Spirit. I want the glory of the Lord."

STUDY QUESTIONS

1. Read I Samuel 18, II Samuel 6:1-23, I Chronicles 15:1-29.

2. Memorize Psalm 30:11,12.

3. Describe the sacred dance in the Scriptures.

4. When are we called to dance before the Lord?

5. Is it a sign of holiness if we don't dance?

6. Did you experience a new liberty when you danced?

CHAPTER FIVE

VICTORY THROUGH THE UPLIFTED HANDS

There is a tremendous power in the upraised hands. The Bible is full of this truth and yet it is one of the great truths which we do not understand. Neither is there much teaching on it. In the Old Testament we read how God's people availed themselves of every avenue that was scriptural in order to have the mighty power of God work in their lives. There is no doubt that God's power was made real to His people when they raised their hands in faith.

I like to see people raise their hands high above their heads. That is the old-time Pentecostal way. The new Charismatic uplift of the hands seems so half-hearted. Probably this is because it is only "half-mast." When a flag flies half-mast it is a sign of death. Let us go beyond the "half-mast" salute and get our hands up higher so we can really praise the Lord and even wave our hands before the Lord as a wave offering unto Him like the priests of old did in the temple of the Lord. (Exodus 29:24)

We Lift Up Our Hands Because We Reverence And Acknowledge The Holy Oracle

Psalm 28:2, *"Hear the voice of my supplications, when I cry unto thee, when I lift up mine hands toward thy holy oracle."*

The holy Oracle is the holy commandments, or the holy Word of God which was given to His people. It probably referred to the tablets whereon the Ten Commandments were written with the hand of God. They were very precious to the Israelites and they were kept in the holy Ark of the Covenant. When people prayed, they would reach their hands out towards it. In this way they acknowledged its sacredness and their reverence to the Word of God.

In John 1:1 and 14 we read that the Word of God became flesh. *"...and the Word was with God, and the Word was God....And the Word was made flesh, and dwelt among us, (and we beheld his glory, the glory as of the only begotten of the Father,) full of grace and truth."* Jesus Christ became the revealed Word of God to us. He is the ORACLE, even the holy Oracle. He no longer resides inside an earthly piece of furniture. He has risen from the dead and ascended to the right hand of God, and that is why, when we worship Him, we raise our hands up, for we are raising them towards the holy Oracle, who is no longer on eye-level, but above us, seated in the heavens with the Father.

It Is An Act Of Body Worship

Do you realize that your body performs acts that portray your emotions? When you clap your hands, you portray your excitement. When you fall prostrate, you portray deep emotion. When you kneel, your portray humility and dependance upon God. When you stand up, you portray readiness to serve or to go. God said the Israelites were to eat the Passover meal standing. This portrayed a readiness to march. When you sit down, it portrays rest and trust. Every act that your body performs is a demonstration of emotion. Dancing expresses great joy.

When you lift up your hands, it is an act of body worship which means that you are worshipping God. Your whole body is worshipping Him, not just your thoughts, not

76

just your heart and spirit, not just your tongue, but your body is worshipping God and because of that, it is a very healthy thing for you to do.

Your Body Acknowledges The Greatness Of God

It is a demonstration that you acknowledge the greatness of God, and that He is above you. He is not your footstool. He has rulership over your life. In the Orient it is considered to be a depraving thing to live in lower land. Those who are someone in power or society always seek to live at a higher elevation.

It Is Like The Offering Of The Evening Sacrifice

Psalm 141:2, *"Let my prayer be set forth before thee as incense; and the lifting up of my hands as the evening sacrifice."* The evening sacrifice was very important. The exact time of the offering of the evening sacrifice is a matter of controversy. But we know that it was offered before the stars came out, at the closing of the day. It spoke of completion. The day was almost finished when the evening sacrifice was offered. It was the final sacrifice of the day that was offered to cover all the sins that had been committed during that day.

According to Jewish custom, the day did not begin in the morning and end at night, but it began when the sun went down. A day was from sundown to sundown. As the priests offered the evening sacrifice, they were asking the Lord to forgive the sins which the nation had committed that very day.

Knowing this truth, you can realize what the lifting up of the hands means. It is an act of evening worship. It is a special sign of drawing close to God for His forgiveness and blessing. It is looking up to God to cover the sins that we have committed knowingly and ignorantly, and getting everything under the Blood. It is an act of turning to the Lord for His protection over us and our family through the hours of the night. That is why it is so good for us, even before we are going to bed, to just stop for a moment at the side of our bed, lift up our hands and say, "Thank You for today, Lord." If you will just stop for a minute and say, "Thank You for this, or thank You for that, cover me with Your Blood, protect me," the lifting of your hands will be as the evening sacrifice. Neither do you need to wait until you go to bed. Any time during the day it is a beautiful act of adoration to God.

When You Lift Your Hands, You Draw Attention To Yourself

When you lift your hands, you draw attention to yourself. Heaven starts to look your way. How many do you think, have even today lifted their hands to God in worship in your city? Perhaps not very many. But you can be so tuned in with God that when you worship Him, and His Spirit comes upon you, you will do those little things that nobody else thinks to do and when you do, God will say, "Look down there, that child of Mine is waving at Me. Now angels, you go down there and bless that one because she is worshipping Me and there are very few in that part of the city that have their hands raised to Me in worship."

You will draw the attention of the armies of heaven to yourself. You will connect with heaven's high voltage power line!

Examples In The Scriptures

The prophets often raised their hands to heaven where God's throne dwells. Let us look at some of the great men of old who raised their hands to God.

Moses: (Exodus 17:8-16) The children of Israel had not been out of Egypt very long before the enemy came against them in the form of the Amalekite army. Israel was defenceless. They had almost no weapons, except for what they might have been able to get from the defeated and drowned Egyptian army. *"And Moses said unto Joshua, Choose us out men, and go out, fight with Amalek: to morrow I will stand on the top of the hill with the rod of God in mine hand. So Joshua did as Moses had said to him, and fought with Amalek. Moses and Aaron and Hur went up to the top of the hill. And it came to pass, when Moses held up his hand, that Israel prevailed: and when he let down his hand, Amalek prevailed."* This is very, very significant.

"But Moses' hands were heavy [in other words, they were tired]*; and they took a stone, and put it under him* [for he had been standing for hours]*, and he sat thereon; and Aaron and Hur stayed* [held] *up his hands, the one on the one side, and the other on the other side; and his hands were steady until the going down of the sun. And Joshua discomfited Amalek and his people with the edge of the sword."* The Lord told Moses to write this testimony for a memorial in a book and rehearse it before the people. He said, *"...I will utterly put out the remembrance of Amalek from under heaven."* That is one way of getting rid of your enemies...just raise your hands to God in full surrender and let Him fight your battle for you.

It was here that Moses built an altar and called it Jehovah-nissi, the Lord is my banner. When Moses raised both his hands, it was like a double ensign. It was a double-portion of power. It was so powerful that all the demonic forces that were arrayed against Israel were put to defeat.

Don't you like to discomfit the devil? That is the opposite of making him "comfortable." When you raise up your hands, you discomfit him. You are disturbing him. You are making him feel like he doesn't want to be around you because he is seeing two "Jehovah-nissis" waving in the air. "The Lord is my banner!" What a beautiful flag we can wave before the enemy! Hallelujah! As we raise our hands, we are really declaring that the Lord is our banner. He is our sign of victory.

When the Queen of England is in residence in Buckingham Palace, her ensign is on the flag pole. When she leaves, it is taken down. When we wave our hands, it is a sign to the world and the devil that the KING is in residence! It brings victory to our spirits, and when the spirit is in victory we have got the victory. The big battles are not fought out there in the "blue yonder," they are fought right here in me. It doesn't make one bit of difference what anybody tries to do to me. If I am living in victory, all the heavens are standing behind me. When I am in victory, I am rising above every situation. There is victory in warfare, victory in the battle, when you lift your hands. God made this truth so real that when Moses' hands came down, Israel began to lose the battle. God was showing us a great truth.

King Solomon prayed with lifted hands: I Kings 8:22-24, *"And Solomon stood before the altar of the Lord in the presence of all the congregation of Israel, and spread forth his hands toward heaven: And he said, Lord God of Israel, there is no God like thee, in heaven above, or on earth beneath, who keepest covenant and mercy with thy* *servants that walk before thee with all their heart: Who hast kept with thy servant David my father that thou promisedst him: thou spakest also with thy mouth, and hast fulfilled it with thine hand, as it is this day."*

Solomon was not reaching toward the holy Oracle, he was looking higher. He was looking into the very gate of heaven because the Lord, the true Oracle had not yet descended. And because He had not yet descended, Solomon, who was the wisest man who ever lived, was really in the Spirit that day. He was not acting according to the laws of the book of Moses, but he was looking up and reaching out into the infinite glory of God, Himself, the Lord, seated high above all the earth on His throne, when he raised his hands and prayed that long prayer which must have taken him many minutes to pray. Solomon was king over all of Israel, and I believe that when we look at Solomon and see how God gave him riches, wisdom and a peaceable reign, we see that in his early years he was the greatest king Israel ever had. God called him to build the holy temple, a thing that He never allowed David to do. And God filled that temple with His glory.

I believe that the reason God blesses us when we lift our hands is because it is a sign of high worship. It is a sign that we are acknowledging that the Lord is bigger than ourselves. And God acknowledges that. It will bring the glory of God into our lives.

Scriptures On The Uplifted Hands

Psalm 134:2, *"Lift up your hands in the sanctuary, and bless the Lord."* This is a command. We obey the other laws and commandments. Why do we ignore this one?

Psalm 63:3,4, *"Because thy lovingkindness is better*

than life, my lips shall praise thee. Thus will I bless thee while I live: I will lift up my hands in thy name." I believe that when we get to heaven, we will see people walking around with their hands lifted up.

I Timothy 2:8, *"I will therefore that men pray every where, lifting up holy hands, without wrath and doubting."*

Paul says that we should always, and in every place feel free to raise our hands in prayer and worship unto the Lord. There are three things about these hands. They are holy hands, they are without wrath and they are confident hands. It is a sign of faith and trust in God. The sinful hands or the bloody hands will not be blessed, rather, they will be judged by the Lord.

Hebrews 12:12, *"Wherefore lift up the hands which hang down..."* The hands of many Christians today look like they are weighted down. They can't lift them up. It also says, *"...and the feeble knees."* This is a two-fold command. The knees speak of intercessory life and the uplifted hand speaks of a life of praise. We need both in order to keep in balance. Some always pray but never praise. Others praise, but never travail in prayer.

The easiest way to receive the Baptism of the Holy Spirit is to begin to praise the Lord. I always lead people, who are seeking to be filled, in a prayer of confession of sin, and then I tell them to praise the Lord.

I remember when the Lord gave me the first touch of glory in my life. I had my hands raised for hours and didn't even realize they were up. When the power of God is upon you, you just want to raise your hands to the Lord in praise and worship.

Luke 24:50,51, *"And he led them out as far as to Bethany, and he lifted up his hands, and blessed them. And it came to pass, while he blessed them, he was parted from them and carried up into heaven.''* The last thing that we see Jesus do, is raise His hands up in blessing. While His hands are lifted up, He is taken up into heaven. That is how Jesus went up!

Martyrs Died With Hands Raised

When we read accounts of how some of our martyrs died, we find that many died with their hands raised to heaven. As Thomas Ridley, the faithful witness, was brought to the stake, the testimony is written of him, "Dr. Ridley, entering the place, marvellous earnestly holding up both hands, looked towards heaven. Then shortly after espying Master Latimer, with a wondrous cheerful look, he ran to him, embraced and kissed him; and as they stood near reported comforted him saying, 'Be of good heart, brother, for God will either assuage the fury of the flame or else strengthen us to abide it.' Then they brought the faggot, kindled with fire, and laid the same down at Dr. Ridley's feet. To whom Master Latimer spake in this manner; 'Be of good comfort, Master Ridley, and play the man. We shall this day light such a candle, by God's grace, in England, as I trust shall never be put out.' "

"When Thomas Cranmer, the Protestant Archbishop of Canterbury was led to the stake, he died a very noble death. Because of the great pressures brought upon him when he was sentenced to be burned to death, he had recanted earlier. This good and great man failed the Lord. But in the very end, as he was supposed to give his renunciatory oration against the faith, he won the victory over the flesh and said, 'And now I come to the great thing that troubleth my conscience more than any other thing that ever I said or did in my life; and this is, the setting abroad things contrary to the truth; which here I now renounce and refuse, as things written with my hand, contrary to the truth which I thought in my heart, and wrote for fear of death, and to save my life, if it might be; and that is, all such bills, which I have written or signed with mine own hand since my degradation; wherein I have written many things untrue. And forasmuch as my hand offended in writing contrary to my heart, therefore my hand shall first be punished; for if I may come to the fire, it shall be first burned.'

"And then Cranmer, being pulled down from the stage, was led to the fire. But when he came to the place where the holy bishops and martyrs of God, Hugh Latimer and Nicholas Ridley, burnt before him for the confession of the truth, kneeling down, he prayed to God and not long tarrying in his prayers, putting off his garments to his shirt, he prepared himself to death. His shirt was made long, down to his feet. His feet were bare; likewise his head, when both his caps were off, was bare, that one hair could not be seen upon it. His beard was long and thick, covering his face with marvellous gravity. Such a countenance of gravity moved the hearts of both his friends and his enemies. Then was an iron chain tied about Cranmer, whom when they perceived to be more steadfast than that he could be moved from his sentence, they commanded the fire to be set unto him.

"And when the wood was kindled and the fire began to burn near him, stretching out his arm, he put his right hand into the flame, which he held so steadfast and immovable, saving that once with the same hand he wiped his face, that all men might see his hand burned before his body was touched. His body did so abide in the burning of the flame which such constancy and steadfastness that standing always in one place without moving his body, he seemed to move no more than the stake to which he was bound; his eyes were lifted up into heaven, and oftentime he repeated 'this unworthy hand,' so long as his voice would suffer him; and using the words of Stephen, 'Lord Jesus, receive my spirit,' in the greatness of the flame he gave up the ghost."

The Protestant Bishop, Robert Ferrar, was a godly man. He too was burned at the stake. It was said of him, "so patiently he stood that he never moved, but he stood holding up his stumps."

All the way from Edinburgh to Wales to London the great men of God and the women of God died in the fires of persecution with their hands raised up to God. It brings blessing, it brings glory, and the gates of glory were lifted for them as they stood there, burning for the name of Jesus Christ and the truth we believe today and which makes us free.

STUDY QUESTIONS

1. Read Exodus 17:8-16.

2. Memorize Psalm 141:2.

3. What does it portray when we lift our hands to God?

4. Why do we draw God's attention to ourselves when we worship Him by raising our hands?

5. Why does Satan get uncomfortable when we raise our hands to the Lord?

The Falling Down of the Walls of Jericho

CHAPTER SIX

VICTORY THROUGH SHOUTING

Let us look at the different Hebrew and Greek words for "shout, shouted," and "shouting" which are used in the Bible.

1. *Anah* (aw-naw), "to sing, shout, testify, announce, cry, etc." (Exodus 32:18)

2. *Teruwah* (ter-oo-aw), "acclamation of joy, battle-cry, clangour of trumpets, alarm, joy, jubilee, loud noise, rejoicing, shouting, high, joyful sound." (Numbers 23:21; Joshua 6:5,20; Ezra 3:11; Psalm 47:1,5; Jeremiah 20:16; Ezekiel 21:22; Zechariah 4:7)

3. *Ruwa* (roo-ah), "to split the ears with sound, shout, blow an alarm, cry aloud, cry out, make a joyful noise, shout for joy, sound an alarm, triumph." (Joshua 6:5; 6:10; II Chronicles 13:15; Psalm 47:1; 65:13; Isaiah 44:23; Jeremiah 50:15; Zephaniah 3:14; Ezra 3:13; Isaiah 16:10)

4. *Ranan* (raw-nan), "to creak, to emit a sound, to shout for joy, cry out, be joyful, to cause to sing aloud for joy and triumph, to squeal with delight." (Psalm 5:11; 132:9; Leviticus 9:24; Psalm 78:65)

5. *Heydad* (hay-dawd), "to shout, acclamation." (Jeremiah 25:30; 51:14; Isaiah 16:9; Jeremiah 48:33)

6. *Tsavach* (tsaw-vakh), "to screech, shout." (Isaiah 42:11)

7. *Tsahal* (tsaw-hal), "to be cheerful, to gleam, to sound clear, to bellow, cry aloud, lift up, neigh (animal expression as well as human)." (Jeremiah 31:7)

8. *Rea* (ray-ah), "a crash of thunder, noise of war, shout of joy." (Exodus 32:17)

9. *Rinnah* (rin-naw), "to shout for joy, to cry out, be

joyful, sing aloud, proclamation of joy." (Proverbs 11:10)

10. *Teshuah* (tesh-oo-aw), "a crashing or loud clamour, crying, noise, shouting, stir." (Zechariah 4:7)

New Testament

11. *Epiphoneo* (ep-ee-fo-neh-o), "to call at something, exclaim, cry, give a shout." (Acts 12:22)

12. *Keleuma* (kelyoo-mah), "a cry of incitement, to urge on, to hail, to order, to bid, to give a command." I Thessalonians 4:16, *"For the Lord himself shall descend from heaven with a shout...."*

The Lord Himself Speaks With A Shout

In the scriptures we can read how the Lord, Himself, has shouted from time to time to reveal Himself and His glory to His people.

Numbers 23:21, *"...the Lord his God is with him, and the shout of a king is among them."* Balaam was hired by Balak to curse Israel, but when he stood up to curse, God's power took his tongue and made him bless Israel instead. God can always turn the curse into a blessing. One of the most beautiful things that Balaam said were these words, "The shout of a king is among them." That King is none other than the King of kings, the Lord of Glory.

If the King lives inside of Israel, then He also lives inside of you. He has brought with Him His shout of triumph and victory. The word used here is *teruwah*, meaning, "acclamation of joy, battle-cry, clangour of trumpets, alarm, joy, jubilee, loud noise, rejoicing, shouting, high, joyful sound." Praise God! God is not afraid to shout the shout of triumph and victory! It is time that we, His children, again begin to

88

sound the battle-cry, and bring back the shout of victory in the camp. Let the enemy know that the King is dwelling among His people!

Psalm 47:5, *"God is gone up with a shout, the Lord with the sound of a trumpet."* He is coming back with a shout and with the sound of the trumpet also. This word for shout is *ruwa* which means "to split the ears with sound, shout, blow an alarm, a loud cry, a joyful noise of triumph." That is our God! He dwells in victory. He is the victory. He went up in victory and He is returning in victory. You and I must go forth in victory also. God is showing His glory through the shout of victory. It will scatter the powers of darkness. They shall be destroyed by the brightness of His coming when He comes back with the ear-splitting shout that will rend the heavens and open the graves of the righteous.

Jeremiah 25:30, *"Therefore prophesy thou against them all these words, and say unto them, The Lord shall roar from on high, and utter his voice from his holy habitation; he shall mightily roar upon his habitation; he shall give a shout, as they that tread the grapes, against all the inhabitants of the earth."* This is the shout of acclamation. God has a big announcement to make to all the world and one of these days we will hear that shout of acclamation. In this scripture God is telling us to prophesy it to happen. Many things are waiting for us to declare it into existance.

Psalm 78:65, *"Then the Lord awaked as one out of sleep, and like a mighty man that shouteth by reason of wine."* The word for shout here is *renan* which means, "to creak, to emit a shrill, grating cry, to squeal with delight, to sing aloud for joy and triumph." It is best-likened to a drunk person roaring around and shouting in an irritating way.

How interesting that God speaks through the psalmist and tells us that after Israel was defeated in warfare and the tabernacle of Shiloh was captured, the glory of God had departed, the priests had fallen, the maidens were without husbands, and everything was lost, that then, He rose up to smite His enemies and when God "woke up," He moved His dwelling place from the territorial tribe of Ephraim to Mount Zion, and He chose the tribe of Judah. When God wakes up with a shout, you can be sure that some big changes are going to take place.

I believe that God has been waiting all these years, with grace and patience for us to change and come into conformity with His will and one of these days He will wake up and there will be a mighty shout that will irritate a lot of people, but it will bring tremendous changes in the workings and movings of God among men. Get ready for it!

Examples Of Shouting In The Scriptures

Joshua is commanded by God to shout: Joshua 6:5, *"And it shall come to pass, that when they make a long blast with the ram's horn, and when ye hear the sound of the trumpet, all the people shall shout with a great shout; and the wall of the city shall fall down flat, and the people shall ascend up every man straight before him."*

God had given the battle-plan to Joshua. It was very important that they obeyed in every detail. They were forbidden to make any noise or say a single word until the day and the moment when God would tell them to shout. They were very obedient and because of their obedience, God could use that stored-up energy and give them a great victory. I wonder what would happen if some of us would be silent for seven days like they were. Of course, they pro-

90

bably spoke the rest of the time, but when they were marching, there was not a word of complaining or grumbling or arguing with their enemies. May God give us this wisdom of SILENCE and SHOUTING. They go hand in hand. There is a time when God's battle-plan for victory is SILENCE.

When the Israelites shouted, the walls of resistance, even the strong fortified walls of Jericho, fell down flat. And from that time the city was cursed. (Joshua 6:17) Such is the power of the Holy Ghost anointed shout of victory. When we start shouting in our dead churches, the walls of tradition will fall down, too!

Does the enemy stand against you and resist everything you do? Do you feel like the battle is not only in vain, but also foolish and ridiculous? Then, why don't you shout at the obstacle and make the enemy look ridiculous instead of yourself!

The battle-cry of victory: II Chronicles 13:13-16, *"But Jeroboam caused an ambushment to come about behind them: so they were before Judah, and the ambushment was behind them. And when Judah looked back, behold, the battle was before and behind: and they cried unto the Lord, and the priests sounded with the trumpets. Then the men of Judah gave a shout: and as the men of Judah shouted, it came to pass, that God smote Jeroboam and all Israel before Abijah and Judah. And the children of Israel fled before Judah: and God delivered them into their hand."*

This was another hopeless situation. Militarily speaking, there was no way that Judah could win against this powerful enemy who had surrounded them in front and behind, but then they remembered the Word of God which He gave to Joshua and while the trumpets sounded, the people shouted with a mighty shout, and God, Himself, came down

91

and fought with Judah and gave them a mighty victory in the battle against their enemy. In fact, 500,000 were slain and cities of people were captured. God still fights the battles of His people.

Why are you losing ground? Is it because you have forgotten to shout the shout of victory? It is time that you enter into all aspects of spiritual warfare.

The word for "shout" used here is *teruwah*, "the battle-cry, clangour of trumpets, alarm, joy, rejoicing, shouting." It is the same as the one used in Joshua 6:5.

When the fire of God fell: Leviticus 9:23, *"And Moses and Aaron went into the tabernacle of the congregation, and came out, and blessed the people: and the glory of the Lord appeared unto all the people. And there came a fire out from before the Lord, and consumed upon the altar the burnt offering and the fat: which when all the people saw, they shouted, and fell on their faces."*

The word here for shout is *rea* (ray-ah) which means, "a crash of thunder, noise of war, shout of victory." It is taken from the root-word *ruwa*, "to split the ears with a loud noise."

You can imagine the shock and the surprise when the fire of God suddenly fell upon the altar and consumed the sacrifice. It was so overwhelming that the people just screamed out; they could not keep silent.

We need to have the fire of God fall again. It will bring back the shout into the camp. Perhaps one reason there is so little shouting of victory in the church today is because it has been a long time since the fire of the Holy Ghost has fallen in our midst. May God send it again. Lord, let the fire fall!

At the laying of the foundation of the temple: Ezra 3:11-13, *"...And all the people shouted with a great shout,*

92

when they praised the Lord, because the foundation of the house of the Lord was laid. But many of the priests and Levites and chief of the fathers, who were ancient men, that had seen the first house, when the foundation of this house was laid before their eyes, wept with a loud voice; and many shouted aloud for joy: So that the people could not discern the noise of the shout of joy from the noise of the weeping of the people: for the people shouted with a loud shout, and the noise was heard afar off."

It was a very emotional scene; one that affected the lives of young and old alike. It was more exciting than the World Series! After 70 years of captivity, they had come home. And now, they were rejoicing in the goodness of God because He had enabled them to begin to rebuild their beloved temple. For the elders of Zion it held many emotional memories. They could remember coming to God's house with their wives and children, most of whom were no longer in the world. For the young, it was the first time that they would ever be able to worship the Lord in His own temple. Can you not imagine how dramatic that must have been! No wonder they shouted! They shouted so loudly that their voice was heard afar off.

Why should we let the world alone release its emotion of joy in the happy sound? It is time that the world knows that we have something to shout about also.

Scriptures About Shouting

Zechariah 4:7, *"Who art thou, O great mountain? before Zerubbabel thou shalt become a plain: and he shall bring forth the headstone thereof with shoutings, crying, Grace, grace unto it."*

This was a prophetic word from the Lord to Zerubbabel, the governor of Judea. God was telling him that even as he had laid the foundation of this house (the temple), he (Zerubbabel) would also finish it. (Verse 9) This was an encouraging word to him, especially when he was hindered by the enemy for many years in completing the task.

Many times God tells us to do something, but Satan hinders us. However, in the end, after all the delay, the victory will be won and the glory and the joy will be so great as we realize that the work we have started, God has helped us to also complete. When we begin to praise the Lord for the victory, we make Satan's triumph turn bitter to him, for we praise the Lord even more because of the answer to prayer that God has given us. The devil will be sorry that he ever interfered to try to stop us.

Turn your defeat into triumph by shouting loud and hard and sincerely and you will do just what the devil did not want you to do.

Psalm 47:1, *"O clap your hands, all ye people; shout unto God with the voice of triumph."* Shouting will bring triumph over all adversity.

Isaiah 12:6, *"Cry out and shout, thou inhabitant of Zion: for great is the Holy One of Israel in the midst of thee."* When we see God's greatness, we have something to shout about.

Isaiah 42:11-14, *"Let the wilderness and the cities thereof lift up their voice, the villages that Kedar doth inhabit: let the inhabitants of the rock sing, let them shout from the top of the mountains. Let them give glory unto the Lord, and declare his praise in the islands. The Lord shall go forth as a mighty man, he shall stir up jealousy like a man of war: he shall cry, yea, roar; he shall prevail against his enemies. I have long time holden my peace; I have been still, and refrained myself: now will I cry like a travailing woman; I will destroy and devour at once."*

When you begin to shout, God begins to rise up and go forth as a mighty man of war. Why doesn't the church of Christ stir up the Lord by shouting? God needs to go to war on our behalf. More is accomplished through shouting and travailing and declaring the Word of the Lord than through a lot of our programming and every man-made effort that we use. We need to find God's battle-plan. Maybe God is waiting for you to give the shout of victory. When you start shouting, God shouts with you. You are never shouting alone.

Zephaniah 3:14,15, *"Sing, O daughter of Zion; shout, O Israel; be glad and rejoice with all the heart, O daughter of Jerusalem. The Lord hath taken away thy judgments, he hath cast out thine enemy: the king of Israel, even the Lord, is in the midst of thee: thou shalt not see evil any more."*

The Lord wants His people Israel to shout the victory and to rejoice with all the heart and as we, His Israel, shout the shout of victory, He will remove the enemy far from us and He will take away the judgments and accusations that Satan has heaped up against us.

Zechariah 9:9, *"Rejoice greatly, O daughter of Zion; shout, O daughter of Jerusalem: behold, thy King cometh unto thee: he is just, and having salvation; lowly, and riding upon an ass, and upon a colt the foal of an ass."*

The Lord commanded in prophecy that the daughter of Zion should shout the welcome to the Messiah. Let us, even now, begin to practice the shout of victory and glory which we will shout as we see Him coming in the clouds of glory. This is the shout that is *ruwa* in Hebrew, even the cry that pierces the ears. Hallelujah! What a shout that will be!

Job 38:7, *"When the morning stars sang together, and all the sons of God shouted for joy?"*

When God laid the foundations of this earth and began His mighty works of creation, the sons of God were shouting. You never know what mighty creative work God will do in your life until you begin to cheer the Lord on by your shouting. What God needs today is real "cheerleaders." He has a lot of complainers and fault-finders. He is looking for those who will volunteer to be His cheerleaders. Will you answer the call?

In Jeremiah 48:33 we read that in Bible times the custom was to tread the wine-press and bring in the harvest with joy and shouting. (Isaiah 16:9,10) When there was no harvest in the time of drought, there was no shouting heard in the fields.

Perhaps, one reason there is so little shouting in the church today is because so few souls are finding the Lord in comparison to the multitudes who are going to hell. It is true that churches are multiplying, but out on the mission fields of the world millions are lost and dying, and there are so few with the burden for their souls. We need a fresh missionary vision today.

I Thessalonians 4:16,17, *"For the Lord himself shall descend from heaven with a shout, with the voice of the archangel, and with the trump of God: and the dead in Christ shall rise first: Then we which are alive and remain shall be caught up together with them in the clouds, to meet the Lord in the air: and so shall we ever be with the Lord."*

This word "shout" is *keleuma* in Greek. It means "a cry to incitement, to urge on, to hail, to order, to bid, to give a command." When the Lord descends with a shout, He will give such a mighty shout that it will bring the righteous out of their graves and call His own from the uttermost parts of the earth. His shout will be a command, like a drill sergeant in the army. We, who know His voice, will hear it and answer that glorious summons. "For the Lord shall descend with a summons to appear before His throne."

The last time that Jesus shouted was when He hung on the cross. *"And at the ninth hour Jesus cried with a loud voice, saying, Eloi, Eloi, lama sabachthani? which is, being interpreted, My God , my God, why hast thou forsaken me?...And the veil of the temple was rent in twain from the top to the bottom."* (Mark 15:34,38)

The last time the Lord Jesus shouted with a loud voice it was so powerful that the veil of the temple was rent in twain. The next time He gives the victory shout, as He descends triumphantly through the heavens, it will rend the heavens and the graves apart and we, who are living and yet remain, will be rent out of the arms and lives of our loved ones who are not ready for the coming of the Lord. Last time He cried, "IT IS FINISHED!" and the earth shook, the rocks were rent and the graves were opened. (Matthew 27:50-52) Think of what will happen when the glorious triumphant King of kings and Lord of lords returns with the victory-shout. And we will all echo back the shout, "I am ready!"

STUDY QUESTIONS

1. Read Numbers 23, Mark 15 and Matthew 27.

2. Memorize I Thessalonians 4:16,17.

3. What is shouting a sign of in the Bible?

4. How can we turn defeat into triumph?

5. What will Jesus' shout at His second coming signify?

CHAPTER SEVEN

VICTORY THROUGH LAUGHING

Isaac means "laughter." He is the father of Israel. Great things are born of laughter. The Hebrew word for Isaac is *yitschaq*.

The Lord laughs. He wants His children to know the power and the secret authority which is theirs when they, too, laugh the laugh of the Lord.

There are different words for laughter in the Hebrew and the Greek. Let us take time to look at them.

1. *Tsachaq* (tsaw-khak), "to laugh outright, (in merriment or scorn), laugh, mock, play, make sport." (Genesis 17:17; 18:13,14; 21:6; Ezekiel 23:32)

2. *Sachaq* (saw-khak), "to laugh (in pleasure or detraction); to deride, have in derision, laugh, make merry, mock, rejoice, laugh to scorn, make sport." (Job 5:22; Proverbs 1:26; Job 12:4, Job 41:29)

3. *Laag* (law-ag), "to deride (as if imitating a foreigner), to speak unintelligibly, have in derision, laugh to scorn, mock."

New Testament

4. *Katagelao* (kat-ag-el-ah-o), "to laugh down, deride, laugh to scorn." (Matthew 9:24; Mark 5:40; Luke 8:53)

5. *Gelao* (ghel-ah-o), "a sign of joy or satisfaction, laughter." (Luke 6:21,25)

From the above we realize there are two distinct kinds of laughter in the Bible. One is a laugh of happiness and the other is a laugh of scorn. God, Himself, laughs both ways. Both are scriptural.

99

God's Humour

God has a very real sense of humour. He even plays tricks on people. God's humour is seen in different stories of the Bible such as these:

Joseph's brothers bowing before Joseph: (Genesis 42:6) After all of Joseph's visions and the cruel way in which they treated him when he told them about his dreams, and after they thought they had "gotten rid of him," it is interesting to see how it all was fulfilled in the end. Compare this scripture with the dream as it is recorded in Genesis 37:9,10.

Pharaoh's daughter adopts Moses: (Exodus 2:10) Pharaoh had ordered the killing of all male children of the Israelites in Egypt, yet God not only spared Moses but Pharaoh became the "adopted grandfather" of one of these sons of Israel. In fact it was the very one who grew up in his palaces and whom he educated and spent money on in food and clothing, etc., who became the deliverer of the children of Israel out of Egypt. When we read this, I wonder whom God is training even now in the Kremlin who will let God's people get out of Russia!

Haman hangs on the gallows he built for Mordecai: (Esther 7:10) Esther was used of God to pin-point the treachery and the evil scheming of Haman to her husband, King Ahasuerus, in such a way that Haman was convicted and executed. But the high point of humour in the story is not the fact that Haman had built the gallows (which he was hung on) for Mordecai, the humorous part is how he comes into the king's chambers the morning after the king has spent a sleepless night and has been reading the account of how Mordecai had saved his life, a thing he had forgotten about. The king immediately wants to reward Mordecai in a special way and give him great honour. At that exact time, (the timing of the Lord is perfect), Haman appears and the king asks him, *"What shall be done unto the man whom the king delighteth to honour?"* (Esther 6:6) Haman thinks the king means himself (Haman) and so he suggests all kinds of things which would please his own ego.

He says, *"Let the royal apparel be brought which the king useth to wear, and the horse that the king rideth upon, and the crown royal which is set upon his head: And let this apparel and horse be delivered to the hand of one of the king's most noble princes, that they may array the man withal whom the king delighteth to honour, and bring him on horseback through the street of the city, and proclaim before him, Thus shall be done to the man whom the king delighteth to honour."* (Esther 6:8,9) He asked for everything but the king's wife. Perhaps this is why the King later accused him of trying to force her (rape her). Esther 7:8, *"Then said the king, Will he force the queen also before me in the house?"* The word "force" (*kabash*) could mean "to violate." The king was not a fool. The intrigue in the oriental courts was always very great. Only a powerful man could stay alive very long. Haman had thought that he was the man to be honoured so he was wishing these things for himself. But the tables turned and all that he had wished for himself was done for the man he hated the most, Mordecai, and he, Haman, was the "most noble prince" who had to dress Mordecai and array him in the royal robes, and bring him through the city, proclaiming, "Thus shall be done unto the man whom the king delighteth to honour."

I have seen God bring into great embarrassment those who have humiliated me. God knows how to turn things around so that you can sit back and laugh with Him at the humorous way that He can pay back your antagonizer for you.

101

The Apostle Peter escapes out of prison: I like to call Peter the great "prison escapee." No one in the Bible ever escaped out of prison as often as he did.

The first time: (Acts 5:17-23) After the miraculous healing of the man at the beautiful gate who had been crippled from birth, revival broke out in Jerusalem. God endowed Peter with such mighty healing power that they brought the sick into the streets and laid them on beds and couches, that at least the shadow of Peter passing by might overshadow some of them. The Bible says, "And they were healed every one." The high priest rose up and all that were with him of the sect of the Sadducees arrested the apostles and put them into the common prison. But at night the angel of the Lord opened the prison doors and brought them forth and told them to go and stand in the temple and keep right on preaching the Gospel. The next morning the officials gathered for the big discussion of what to do with Peter and when they called for the soldiers to bring him up before the council, they found that he was not there, though the prison was shut with all security and the keepers were standing guard, but the prisoner was missing. As they heard this report with shock, someone arrived with a further report that Peter was even now preaching the Gospel in the temple. Glory to God! It is impossible to keep an anointed man from God's calling in his life.

The second time: (Acts 12:1-17) Again we see Peter miraculously delivered from prison on the night before he was supposed to be executed. There was a great excitement at the prison the next morning and Herod examined the keepers, and commanded them to be put to death, putting the blame on them. God in the heavens laughed at them because He knew that He had the keys to the prisons. God is so positively in control of every situation of the lives that are dedicated to Him that He can laugh at adversity. When we are dedicated to Him, we can laugh with God.

Scriptures About God Laughing

Psalm 37:12,13, *"The wicked plotteth against the just,...The Lord shall laugh at him: for he seeth that his day is coming."*

The word for "laugh" here is translated from the Hebrew word *sachaq* which means "to deride, have in derision, mock, laugh to scorn, make sport of."

It will be a terrible day for the wicked when the God of mercy begins to mock and make sport of him. The world has never known that kind of a God but that day is coming.

Psalm 59:7,8, *"...swords are in their lips: for who, say they, doth hear?   But thou, O Lord, shalt laugh at them; thou shalt have all the heathen in derision."*

We tremble at those who have "swords in their mouth" but there is no need to fear, for their day is coming and in that day God will laugh at them.   If the Lord is in us, we can already know that the enemy is defeated and we can laugh at the sword in his mouth.

Examples Of Laughter In The Bible

Abraham: Genesis 17:15-17, *"And God said unto Abraham, As for Sarai thy wife, thou shalt not call her name Sarai, but Sarah shall her name be.   And I will bless her, and give thee a son also of her: yea, I will bless her, and she shall be a mother of nations; kings of people shall be of her. Then Abraham fell on his face and laughed...."*

The words of the Lord made Abraham laugh so hard that he lost complete control of himself.   He fell on his face,

103

lay prostrate on the ground, and shook with laughter. He must have had a good imagination, for his next words reveal just what he was thinking. *"Shall a child be born unto him that is an hundred years old? and shall Sarah, that is ninety years old bear?"* He was seeing his old body and Sarah's old body. And the whole thing seemed ludicrous to him.

The time has come for God to give us promises that will seem just as ridiculous and absurd. Things are going to happen in these days that will "slay us with laughter." God renewed both Sarah's and Abraham's bodies. She not only gave birth to Isaac, she also breast-fed him. And then she lived many more years. She was 127 when she died; so she lived another 37 years after that. That is one generation of time. After her death, at the age of 137, Abraham married Keturah and she bare him six more sons. (Genesis 25:1,2) He died at the age of 175, after seeing his son's children. Isaac was 60 years old when Rebekah bore him Esau and Jacob (Genesis 25:26) and that made Abraham 160 years of age at that time. The twins were about 15 years old when the Lord took Abraham home. For 75 years of his life Abraham could laugh at the miracle power of God's resurrection life in his body. Every time he called the name, "Isaac," he was saying, "laughter." God wants us to have an eternal sense of humour. He wants us to laugh at our debts, our sicknesses, our dried up bodies, our enemies, our dry pastures, our old age, and every hard situation in our lives. God is laughing at them, why don't we join in and laugh with Him? I believe that laughter is like medicine and it will lengthen our days on the earth. Proverbs 17:22, *"A merry heart doeth good like a medicine: but a broken spirit drieth the bones."*

The word "drieth" in the above verse comes from the Hebrew word *yabesh* which means, "to dry up, confuse, confound, shame, wither away."

The word "bones" comes from *etsem*, meaning, "the body, the strength, the bones."

Many people lose their strength because they lose their joy. That is why the word of the Lord says, *"...Sara herself received strength to conceive seed,..."* (Hebrews 11:11) Her heart was filled with joy and laughter, for Sarah laughed too.

Sarah: Genesis 18:12, *"Therefore Sarah laughed within herself, saying, After I am waxed old shall I have pleasure, my lord being old also?"* This word, "pleasure" (*eden* or *ednah* in the Hebrew) means "delicate, delight, pleasure." It is the same word as "Eden," the Garden of Eden.

When we begin to laugh, the Lord brings us back into that Garden of Eden experience where "all things are new." There was only joy and harmony and eternal life in the Garden until sin entered in. But Jesus died and took upon Himself our sin and condemnation so that the curse was laid upon Him and we today can enter again into the garden of holy joy and pleasure, even the Garden of Eden, and together with Sarah, we can become participants of our inheritance, the partakers of joy, even as our first parents were and as Abraham and Sarah became in their old age. We shall yet bring forth fruit in old age when the joy of the Lord is our strength.

The daughters of Zion laughed the enemy, Sennacherib, King of Assyria to scorn: II Kings 19:21, *"This is the word that the Lord hath spoken concerning him; The virgin the daughter of Zion hath despised thee, and laughed thee to scorn; the daughter of Jerusalem hath shaken her head at thee."*

When the enemy came against Jerusalem, King Hezekiah was in great consternation. To make things even worse, the enemy wrote him a letter filled with threats and mockery. When he received it and read it, he went up into the house of the Lord, and spread it before the Lord. That is a good thing to do with all accusations that come from the devil. The Lord spoke to him and comforted him and sent a message to him through Isaiah, the prophet, in which were these words to the enemy, "The virgin the daughter of Zion hath despised thee, and laughed thee to scorn; the daughter of Jerusalem hath shaken her head at thee." God saw into the future just what would happen and He announced it as a thing that had already happened. God wants us to look into His finished work and see His answer to our prayer and envision things as they will be when He has finished working out every problem and every situation which is threatening us now. God saw the women laugh. I believe that God today looks at His daughters who are going through trials and testings and He is already hearing them laugh the laugh of victory. Why don't you join Him?

The leviathan laughs at his enemy: Job 41:29, *"Darts are counted as stubble: he laugheth at the shaking of a spear."* Praise God! I believe that there is a covering in God where we are so hidden in the cleft of the Rock that the darts that the enemy throws at us are counted as stubble, and we can laugh at him when he shakes the spear at us. God describes the leviathan in such a way that we are to realize that in Him we are that same powerful new creation that cannot be destroyed by the evil one.

Scriptures On Laughter

Ecclesiastes 3:4, *"A time to weep, and a time to laugh...."*

Yes, there is a time when we must let the laughter of the

106

Lord fill our hearts. If we are to allow God to laugh, then He must laugh through us, just like He speaks through us.

There is a holy laughter in the Spirit when we laugh at God's victory over evil and see the humour of God. It is God laughing in us.

Psalm 52:6, *"The righteous also shall see, and fear, and shall laugh at him."* Because we can see in the Spirit the power and the final workings of God and we have respect and reverence for Him we can laugh at the enemy.

Job 8:20,21, *"Behold, God will not cast away a perfect man, neither will he help the evil doers: Till he fill thy mouth with laughing, and thy lips with rejoicing."* God says here that you will have a good laugh when you see what God will do with your enemy. God will not cast you away, neither will He help the evil doer. God is staging a comedy before your very eyes, so that you can laugh with Him at the victory which He has planned for you. The script has been written, the show is in progress; relax and enjoy the drama in joyous anticipation of the victorious finale!

Psalm 126:2, *"Then was our mouth filled with laughter, and our tongue with singing: then said they among the heathen, The Lord hath done great things for them."* When we begin to laugh, it will be a great witness before all non-believers and doubters. It will prove to them the great confidence which we have in God.

There are many scriptures against laughter in Ecclesiastes such as Ecclesiastes 2:2; 7:3,6; 10:19. These seem to refute what the rest of the Word of God says, but remember that Ecclesiastes is "carnal man" speaking.

Rejoicing Is A Part Of Laughter

It is impossible to have laughter without joy. God will

107

not only give you joy when you begin to laugh, but He will also cause your joy to be portrayed by laughter. There are very many scriptures on rejoicing. Let us just mention a few of them.

Psalm 5:11,12, *"But let all those that put their trust in thee rejoice: let them ever shout for joy, because thou defendest them: let them also that love thy name be joyful in thee. For thou, Lord, wilt bless the righteous; with favour wilt thou compass him as with a shield."*

When we begin to rejoice in the Lord it puts a shield around about us and protects us from the evil that can happen to our heart. Joy and worry cannot go together.

Deuteronomy 12:7, *"And there ye shall eat before the Lord your God, and ye shall rejoice in all that ye put your hand unto, ye and your households, wherein the Lord thy God hath blessed thee."* God wants His people to have times of celebration and rejoicing when their mouths can be "filled with laughter." That is one reason He appointed feast days.

Deuteronomy 16:11, *"And thou shalt rejoice before the Lord thy God, thou, and thy son, and thy daughter, and thy manservant, and thy maidservant, and the Levite that is within thy gates, and the stranger, and the fatherless, and the widow, that are among you, in the place which the Lord thy God hath chosen to place his name there."* God wants EVERYONE to rejoice and have a BIG PARTY in Him. He does not want to exclude anyone, neither the servant, nor the handmaiden, nor the widow, nor the orphan, nor the stranger...and not even the priest. God doesn't want the priest to go around with a long face and a show of piety. He would rather see him laughing and dancing and praising the Lord.

Zechariah 9:9, *"Rejoice greatly, O daughter of Zion...."*

God wants you to be happy in what He is doing. He is coming to you. Rejoice!

Luke 10:20, *"...but rather rejoice, because your names are written in heaven."* Jesus told us to rejoice because our names were recorded in heaven. Isn't it wonderful to know that YOUR name is written in the book of life up there, together with the great saints like Paul, Peter, Lydia, Dorcas, Abraham and Sarah? That is something to really rejoice over.

Romans 12:15, *"Rejoice with them that do rejoice...."* Give of yourself. Don't pull yourself away from happy people and separate yourself in your misery.

Philippians 4:4, *"Rejoice in the Lord alway: and again I say, Rejoice."* God wants you to have a continual feast of joy. We have been taught that sadness is more spiritual. But this is not scriptural. God wants us to be a happy people and a joyful people.

I Thessalonians 5:16, *"Rejoice evermore."*

When Should We Rejoice?

Neither should we wait for good times before we can rejoice. We can rejoice under all circumstances because the Lord is the source of our joy and not our circumstances. We can rejoice in:

1. Famine: *"Although the fig tree shall not blossom, neither shall fruit be in the vines; the labour of the olive shall fail, and the fields shall yield no meat; the flock shall be cut off from the fold, and there shall be no herd in the stalls: Yet I will rejoice in the Lord, I will joy in the God of my salvation. The Lord God is my strength, and he will make my feet like hinds' feet, and he will make me to walk upon mine high places..."* (Habakkuk 3:17-19) This is the

song of victory in the time of famine.

2. In time of persecution: *"Blessed be ye, when men shall hate you, and when they shall separate you from their company, and shall reproach you, and cast out your name as evil, for the Son of man's sake. Rejoice ye in that day, and leap for joy: for, behold, your reward is great in heaven: for in the like manner did their fathers unto the prophets."* (Luke 6:22,23)

3. In suffering: *"Who now rejoice in my sufferings for you...."* (Colossians 1:24) The Lord draws very close when we suffer for Him and for others.

4. In the loss of possessions: *"For ye had compassion of me in my bonds, and took joyfully the spoiling of your goods, knowing in yourselves that ye have in heaven a better and an enduring substance."* (Hebrews 10:34)

In the original Greek it would read, "You allowed with joy the plundering (or snatching away) of your belongings, knowing that you have a treasure in heaven which is better and remains." We are living in days when we can lose everything, and I myself have lost all my possessions three times in my life, but never was I saddened by the loss, for the Lord told me long ago, *"...a man's life consisteth not in the abundance of the things which he possesseth."* (Luke 12:15)

5. In fiery trials: *"Beloved, think it not strange concerning the fiery trial which is to try you, as though some strange thing happened unto you: But rejoice, inasmuch as ye are partakers of Christ's sufferings; that, when his glory shall be revealed, ye may be glad also with exceeding joy. If ye be reproached for the name of Christ, happy are ye; for the spirit of glory and of God resteth upon you...."* (I Peter 4:12-14) There is a certain kind of very great glory that only comes when we are enduring unexplainable and strange

fiery trials. This trial brings its own kind of spiritual joy and happiness and it is the most difficult of all tests because we, ourselves, cannot understand what it is all about or why it has happened to us. If we could understand and explain why, it wouldn't be half so difficult to bear. But later on we will understand why.

Rejoicing and laughter drives out self-pity. Self-pity is one of Satan's most effective weapons. He is very skilful at using it against the saints of God.

People Who Rejoiced In The Bible

1. Miriam (Exodus 15:20,21)
2. Hannah (I Samuel 2:1,11,15)
3. David (II Samuel 6:14-16)
4. Mary (Luke 1:47)
5. The angels (Luke 2:13)
6. The eunuch (Acts 8:39)
7. Paul and Silas' prison warden (Acts 16:34)
8. Peter and John (Acts 5:41)
9. Paul in prison (Acts 16:23,25)

And of course, there are very many more.

Pat Parks' Testimony

Just recently, one of our End-Time Handmaidens, Pat Parks, who is a neighbour of ours, had a great victory over the tricks of Satan by laughing at the devil. I have asked her to share this testimony with you. Here it is:

"I had received a cheque in the mail that was to go towards Judy Bare's and my trip to Texas and California where we had meetings scheduled.

"Friday morning on March 23, 1984 I decided to go to

111

the bank with the cheque. However, just before I left, I laid the cheque under a letter on the kitchen bar. I went to the back of the house for a minute to attend to something and when I came back to pick up the cheque and letter, the cheque was gone! Immediately, I knew the devil had stolen it. (Pat was alone in the house at that time.)

"Well, you know, thoughts come to your mind, you hear, 'No, you just misplaced it.' Knowing full well I hadn't, I looked anyway...in drawers, trashbaskets, all the rooms, etc. This went on for an hour and as I looked, I prayed, took authority over Satan, and praised God, knowing the enemy had to return that cheque.

"Finally, I called Engeltal (the headquarters of the End-Time Handmaidens), and related to Myrna (one of our secretaries) what had taken place and she prayed over the phone and we stood in agreement.

"Later, talking to Sister Gwen, I found out that while they were still in devotions, and just before they received my phone call, the Holy Spirit had given Sister Gwen a burden for our finances. So they prayed at that moment. When they were through praying, Myrna walked into the chapel and related to everyone that I had just called and she shared the incident about the stolen cheque and they prayed again.

"I continued to pray another hour and told Satan he had "goofed" again, for instead of me feeling defeated, I felt victorious and he had only managed to really get me on the 'war path' after him and new determination came over me to destroy his kingdom of darkness.

"At one point, I was sitting on the bar stool and just on the other side of the wall, which would be the outside of the house, a bird came and pecked extremely hard against the house. Then it moved a few inches to the stained glass window in the dining room and began to peck hard against it, to the point, I became concerned that the window would break, and if it had, it would indeed have been expensive to replace.

"One doesn't need to be a prophet to know that this was harassment and there was a connection between the incident with the stolen cheque and the bird.

"Then the Lord led me to do a different kind of warfare against the enemy. Now He has taught me to rebuke, take authority and enter into praise and worship to combat the "ole boy." However, after having done all the above I just mentioned, and still missing the cheque, a thought came to me like a light, 'Laugh at the devil!' The Lord gave me the scripture, Psalm 2:4, *"He that sitteth in the heavens shall laugh: the Lord shall have them in derision."* (Are we in the heavens with the Lord?)

"So I laughed. I laughed so much that the joy of the Lord overtook me to the point that if there had been someone observing me with the carnal mind, they would have thought me to be a bit touched in the head.

"The Spirit then led me to walk out of the house to our deck at the front of our home and to laugh even more. What joy I experienced! I was even thankful for what had happened, for I knew the outcome of this battle. I was the winner. I was the head and not the tail.

"While laughing, my eye caught the edge of a paper and as I turned to look, there was the cheque, stuck between a board of the deck and the front of the house!

"Now, bear in mind, I had not been outside of the house earlier. The door had not been unlocked for the day until I went out to laugh at Satan!!! I went back into the house, cheque in hand, and filled the house once again with praises.

"When Judy, my co-worker and friend, returned from the trip, she remarked that when she came in on our road, even before she had arrived on our property, she sensed a cleansing in the spiritual realm had taken place in our area, as well as on the property. I shared with her the battle that had taken place that day.

"I cannot end this testimony without sharing perhaps the most important part of it all. For truly it is one of the main keys of the kingdom of God in living an overcoming life.

"That morning, in the early hours, I had been in very high praise and worship with the Lord. The devil hates worship and he will oppose a worshipper of the Lord. But I wonder if I had not been with Jesus in the holy place that morning, before the battle took place, would I have felt and experienced the victory in that particular battle? Had I not been in the secret chamber with the heavenly Bridegroom, would I have been able to win so glorious a victory?"

STUDY QUESTIONS

1. Read Esther 6,7, Genesis 17,18, II Kings 18,19.

2. Memorize Job 8:20,21.

3. Did you ever experience the humour of God in your own life?

4. What affect does laughing have on us?

5. Why can we rejoice in fiery trials?

6. Who did God command to keep the feast days?

CHAPTER EIGHT

VICTORY THROUGH MARCHING AND WALKING

There is no doubt that there is a certain miraculous power connected with walking or marching over property. The first we hear about it, is when God told Abraham to walk through the length and breadth of the land.

Abraham

Genesis 13:17, *"Arise, walk through the land in the length of it and in the breadth of it; for I will give it unto thee."*

Psalm 24:1 says, *"The earth is the Lord's, and the fulness thereof; the world, and they that dwell therein."* God has the right to give any parcel of land to any people at any time that He pleases. Men are only tenants, (or should I say, squatters?)

Even if we live four-score years or more, when we die it is no more ours. But God wants us to know that if He has a piece of land that He wants to put us in charge of to be supervisors over, He has many ways and means of putting it under our care. We are only His stewards but if we are faithful, we can possess it for a lifetime.

When God told Abraham to walk through the land of the Canaanites, He was giving him the key of possession. He was showing us all how to claim that which He wants to give to us. It was over 400 years later that this land came into the possession of the children of Abraham, but God never forgot the covenant He had made with Abraham. When Abraham began to walk on the land, it was the same as signing the deed of ownership with God.

116

Israel

Over 400 years later God again spoke to Israel, reconfirming the promise to them through the same token of ownership. God said to Isaiah: *"For if ye shall diligently keep all these commandments which I command you, to do them, to love the Lord your God, to walk in all his ways, and to cleave unto him; Then will the Lord drive out all these nations from before you, and ye shall possess greater nations and mightier than yourselves. Every place whereon the soles of your feet shall tread shall be your's: from the wilderness and Lebanon, from the river, the river Euphrates, even unto the uttermost sea shall your coast be. There shall no man be able to stand before you: for the Lord your God shall lay the fear of you and the dread of you upon all the land that ye shall tread upon, as he hath said unto you."* (Deuteronomy 11:22-25)

God made a conditional covenant with Israel. The condition was that they would **love the Lord and obey His commandments and walk in His ways.** Only if we walk in His ways can we possess the land that the soles of our feet tread upon. It takes holy living to obtain holy promises. Many want to claim the promises of God, but they do not live according to their covenant relationship with God and then they wonder why their prayers are unanswered.

Joshua

The Word of God says, *"Now after the death of Moses the servant of the Lord it came to pass, that the Lord spake unto Joshua the son of Nun, Moses' minister, saying, Moses my servant is dead; now therefore arise, go over this Jordan, thou, and all this people, unto the land which I do give to them, even to the children of Israel. Every place that the sole of your foot shall tread upon, that have I given unto you, as I said unto Moses. From the wilderness and this Lebanon even unto the great river, the river Euphrates, all the land of the Hittites, and unto the great sea toward the going down of the sun, shall be your coast. There shall not any man be able to stand before thee all the days of thy life: as I was with Moses, so I will be with thee: I will not fail thee, nor forsake thee."* (Joshua 1:1-5)

This is a glorious confirmation of possession to Joshua which was identical in many ways to the one He had given to all of Israel, but now He was identifying Joshua as His recognized leader of Israel.

God is saying, "When you walk the land, the soles of your feet touch the soil, you are 'staking out your claim.' " I believe that much "land remaineth to be possessed." We have allowed the enemy to usurp authority over the rightful owners who are the true citizens of the Kingdom. But the day has come when the Lord wants us to rise up and possess our inheritance. God is saying to us, as He said to Joshua, *"Only be thou strong and very courageous, that thou mayest observe to do according to all the law, which Moses my servant commanded thee: turn not from it to the right hand or to the left, that thou mayest prosper whithersoever thou goest."* (Joshua 1:7) He goes on to say, *"...for then thou shalt make thy way prosperous, and then thou shalt have good success...be not afraid, neither be thou dismayed: for the Lord thy God is with thee whithersoever thou goest."* It is time for us to "take a walk with God" and stake out our claim for His Kingdom. The kingdoms of this world must now become the kingdoms of our God and His Christ. (Revelation 11:15) He has redeemed it from the curse for His own.

118

I firmly believe that one of the greatest "spiritual battle-plans" that God has given us has remained untried, and that is to literally walk over the territory and claim it for God. If it was not important, why did God tell Abraham to walk over the land of the Hittites and claim it? God does nothing without a purpose. Let us get back to the Bible pattern!

God Walked In The Garden

Genesis 3:8 says, *"And they heard the voice of the Lord God walking in the garden in the cool of the day...."* God would come down and walk in the garden with Adam and Eve. It brought His glory down upon this planet.

God Walked Out Of Egypt With His People

God has always "walked" with His people. In the wilderness the children of Israel were not alone. Psalm 68:7,8 says, *"O God, when thou wentest forth before thy people, when thou didst march through the wilderness; Selah: The earth shook, the heavens also dropped at the presence of God: even Sinai itself was moved at the presence of God, the God of Israel. Thou, O God, didst send a plentiful rain, whereby thou didst confirm thine inheritance, when it was weary."* When God walked with His people in the wilderness, significant things happened. The very earth shook, the heavens dipped low, rain clouds gathered and there was rain. When we pray and seek the face of God, He walks with us and sends the spiritual rain as well as the natural rain over us.

May God help us to "walk with God through the nations and bring Holy Ghost rain upon the dry nations.

There has never been such spiritual drought as there is now. God is calling us to walk and march and travel through the nations of the world, bringing the clouds of glory and the latter rain with us. I believe this is why so many Christians are touring about and making trips to different nations. God is sending them to Russia, to Israel, to India and even to Red China. He is calling them to possess the land Some will never preach or hold big meetings, but they are the "salt of the earth" and when they come, they bring that "salt" with them.

God Walked In The Camp With His People

Deuteronomy 23:14, *"For the Lord thy God walketh in the midst of thy camp, to deliver thee, and to give up thine enemies before thee; therefore shall thy camp be holy: that he see no unclean thing in thee, and turn away from thee."* God told Israel that they must keep the camp clean. He gave them rules of cleanliness and sanitation. First He said that the people should take a bath when they came into the camp in the evening. (Deuteronomy 23:11) Then He told them that they must use a special place outside of the camp for the public toilet and that they were to keep that area covered, that no uncleanness be seen at any time. God said that He was walking in the camp, protecting them from their enemy, and if He would see anything that was unclean, He would turn away from them.

I wonder, as God walks in our houses and our "camps" (or churches), does He see uncleanness that turns Him away from us? What does He see when He looks at our magazine-rack? What does He see when we turn on our T.V.? Do we have in our homes uncleanness which drives God away? God also loves order. He hates confusion and a messy house or yard. I believe that it is time women are taught to keep their homes clean and orderly, so that God can walk in their midst. A messy house is no indication of spirituality, unless it be in a negative way. An unclean person and an unclean and messy dwelling, office or place of work often reveals an unclean demonic spirit is in residence there. Let us clean up the place where we live and where we work, for God is walking in our midst.

Quiet My Spirit In The North Country

In Zechariah 6:1-8 we read an interesting vision that God gave to His prophet Zechariah.

Zechariah saw four chariots pulled by horses go out into the directions of the four winds. When he did not understand what this vision meant, the angel told him, *"...These are the four spirits of the heavens, which go forth from standing before the Lord of all the earth."* (Zechariah 6:5) He said that they went to and fro through the earth. They did this at the command of the Lord, *"...Get you hence, walk to and fro through the earth...."* (Verse 7) God said that the reason for it was, *"Behold, these that go toward the north country have quieted my spirit in the north country."* (Verse 8)

Next time there is trouble in your church or in your household or ministry, why don't you try walking the territory and claiming God's Spirit to quiet the place and bring peace? Drive out the evil spirits from your territory.

The reason that God had to send the "messengers of peace" into the north country was because Israel's enemies always came from the north. Even to this day, Israel's enemies are mostly to the north of Israel. God knows where your enemies are and He will send out His "cavalry" to "quiet things down."

If you cannot walk over a certain territory in the physical way, if you can cover it with your prayers and "walk in the Spirit" over the territory that you are claiming, it will be just as effective.

Walk About Zion!

In Psalm 48:12 God says, *"Walk about Zion, and go round about her: tell the towers thereof."* The word "tell" in Hebrew is *iscaphar*, "to score with a mark, as a tally, or record, to inscribe, to enumerate, to celebrate, to count, to declare, to show forth."

God rejoices when His people "take another look" at the great things that He has done for them. The song writer puts it in these words:

"Count your blessings—name them one by one;
Count your blessings—see what God has done;
Count your blessings—name them one by one;
Count your many blessings—see what God has done."

I believe that if we would start "counting" the land-marks in our lives, we would truly rejoice and praise God and begin to gain even more territorial rights for the Kingdom of God.

How We Must Walk

It is important that we walk in the right way.

1. Walk in faith (Romans 4:12)
2. Walk in newness of life (Romans 6:4)

3. Walk in the Spirit (Galatians 5:16)
4. Walk in love (Ephesians 5:2)
5. Walk as children (Ephesians 5:8).

Enoch Walked With God

Enoch had the right attitude and the right spirit. *"And Enoch walked with God: and he was not; for God took him."* (Genesis 5:24) Enoch walked right into the Kingdom of God. There is a walk that is on a very high spiritual plane. May God help each one of us to walk in that high realm with Him!

Ruth, The Moabitess

When Ruth came to Bethlehem, she was only a widowed "beggar," the poorest of the poor. But she went out to glean in the fields of Boaz. As she walked through the fields, she was making the first steps in claiming them as her own.

The first step in being a successful missionary is to "walk and claim the mountains." *"How beautiful upon the mountains are the feet of him that bringeth good tidings, that publisheth peace; that bringeth good tidings of good, that publisheth salvation; that saith unto Zion, Thy God reigneth!"* (Isaiah 52:7)

When we walk to and fro throughout the land, we are claiming the territory for God. Hebrews 2:8 says, *"Thou hast put all things in subjection under his feet..."* Christ is in us and therefore, all things are under our feet when He lives in our lives. Let us take the dominion. He has paid the price for it.

End-Time Handmaiden Delivers Many Lives From Death

In June 1983 God spoke to our End-Time Handmaiden, Ruth Long, who lives in Coalinga, California, and told her to begin to walk the streets of her little city by night and to pray over the city. He also told her prayer-partner to do the same thing. So in obedience to the leading of the Holy Ghost, they began walking down every street and alley in the entire town. They came home with their feet tired and sore. The next night they decided they would drive instead. But the Lord dealt with them that this was not His will. He wanted them to walk through the city and not drive about in their car.

They covered the downtown section at least 25-30 times. The last ten days they felt a great unrest in the Spirit and they prayed with great fervency, not knowing what was the matter. Then the earthquake struck their city! The downtown area was almost completely destroyed. People said that it was an absolute miracle that no one had been killed. I believe that the city was spared because these two daughters of the Lord claimed every square foot that they walked on.

Intercession Prevents Tornado

Recently, I heard about a man who daily walked the streets of Malvern, Arkansas. He was not a church-goer, but every day he walked all over Malvern, praying for its safety. And though southern Arkansas is a natural spawning ground for tornadoes, they had never been touched by one in that city. When the man died, it seemed that God had no one to take his place as an intercessor for the city. Two days before Christmas a killer tornado struck the city, leaving millions of dollars worth of damage.

God spoke to different ones to walk through their cities, their towns and even their nations. God is working in mysterious ways these days. We may not understand what it is all about, but I believe that when the soles of our feet tread upon a certain place in the will of God, that the Lord can give us that place either spiritually or naturally, and perhaps even in both ways.

Ruth, the Moabitess, did not realize, as she went out to glean in the fields, that she would one day be the mistress of the entire fields and that her son who would come from her womb would be the next owner of the fields which she gleaned. I believe that in the millenium many missionaries will return to their mission fields to reign over them as the Lord's governors and governesses.

"Arise, walk through the land in the length of it and in the breadth of it; for I will give it unto thee." (Genesis 13:17)

STUDY QUESTIONS

1. Read Genesis 13, Joshua 1.

2. Memorize Genesis 13:17.

3. Is there a condition to our possessing God's promises?

4. What is His "key of possession?"

5. What keeps God from walking with us?

6. What are the five ways in which we must walk?

CHAPTER NINE

VICTORY THROUGH CLAPPING

The clapping of the hands is another weapon for victory.

Psalm 47:1 says, *"O clap your hands, all ye people; shout unto God with the voice of triumph."*

When people clap their hands, it is an expression of joy, appreciation, applause, encouragement and greeting. In some nations people do not knock on the door of the house when they come to visit, they clap their hands. In China, when people have finished eating in a restaurant and want the attention of the waiter, they clap their hands. It is done to draw attention.

It is scriptural for God's people to clap their hands to God in appreciation to Him for His greatness and His goodness.

The Waters Clap Their Hands

The psalmist says in Psalm 98:8, *"Let the floods clap their hands: let the hills be joyful together."* The Lord is likening the sound of the waves of the sea unto the clapping of hands. And sometimes this truly describes what it sounds like when the waves lap against the shore.

The Trees Of The Fields Clap Their Hands

Isaiah 55:12, *"For ye shall go out with joy, and be led forth with peace: the mountains and the hills shall break forth before you into singing, and all the trees of the field shall clap their hands."*

This word for "clap" comes from the Hebrew *macha*, which means "to rub, to strike the hands together in exultation, to clap."

It is an act of triumph, jubilation and rejoicing. God is saying that when we go forth in joy, we cause our joy to fall upon all of creation and soon the creation of God, the trees, respond to our happiness, and they too, in their own way, exalt the Lord in jubilation. Why is it that certain people are better at growing plants than others? Is it that they have the capacity to share their inner joy with the plant life? Maybe they can even communicate to the plants something which they cannot communicate to people.

Clapping — An Expression Of Distain

Lamentations 2:15, *"All that pass by clap their hands at thee...."* It was also a sign of mockery and distain when people clapped their hands at Jerusalem. When the Lord calls us to clap our hands, it can have two purposes:

1. To praise and applaud the Lord,
2. To mock at the devil and his evil spirits.

I have often heard the priests and idol worshippers clapping their hands at funerals and in temples and different places of worship. This is because they recognize that clapping the hands chases devils away. This is an ancient oriental custom and I am sure that this was one aspect of it in Bible times and one of the reasons God encourages His people to clap their hands. Besides, when you praise the Lord, you put the devil to scorn.

127

Stamping The Foot

"Thus saith the Lord God; Smite with thine hand, and stamp with thy foot, and say, Alas for all the evil abominations of the house of Israel! for they shall fall by the sword, by the famine, and by the pestilence." (Ezekiel 6:11)

God told the prophet, Ezekiel, to "act out" the judgment that was going to come upon Israel because of her sins. It was not a foolish thing to do, it was ordered by the Lord. It is scriptural therefore to "smite with the hand" (clap) and to stamp with our feet against the enemy. He has given us enough trouble, let us trouble him too.

They Clapped Their Hands At The Coronation Of The King

II Kings 11:12, *"And he brought forth the king's son, and put the crown upon him, and gave him the testimony; and they made him king, and anointed him; and they clapped their hands, and said, God save the king."*

When we clap our hands to the Lord, we are applauding Him as King of our lives! I believe that there will be clapping of the hands as a sign of victory and adoration in heaven. But why wait until we get to heaven? Let us join with creation and applaud the Lord of glory even now by the clapping of our hands. "O clap your hands, all ye people!"

Ten-Stringed Instrument

Remember that David said, *"Praise the Lord with harp: sing unto him with the psaltery and an instrument of ten strings."* (Psalm 33:2)

128

Many teachers of the Word of God like to liken the ten-stringed instrument of this verse with the ten fingers of the hands. And it is true that we can use our ten fingers as instruments unto the Lord.

STUDY QUESTIONS

1. Memorize Psalm 47:1 and Isaiah 55:12.

2. What are the two different expressions of clapping our hands?

3. What can our hands be likened to?

CHAPTER TEN

VICTORY THROUGH HISSING

This may seem a strange thing to do. But the Bible also tells of God telling His people to hiss at the enemy.

In I Kings 9:8 we read, *"And at this house, which is high, every one that passeth by it shall be astonished, and shall hiss; and they shall say, Why hath the Lord done thus unto this land, and to this house?"* This is a prophecy the Lord spoke through King Solomon on the day of the dedication of the temple. He warned his people that if they would turn from following Him and go after other gods, they would become an astonishment, a hissing and a curse. (Jeremiah 25:9,18; 29:18; 51:37) Later, this is just what happened.

In Lamentations 2:15 we read, *"All that pass by clap their hands at thee; they hiss and wag their head at the daughter of Jerusalem, saying, Is this the city that men call The perfection of beauty, The joy of the whole earth?"*

People actually did fulfil this prophecy given by King Solomon 400 years after it was given.

The Wicked Shall Be Hissed At

Job 27:23, *"Men shall clap their hands at him, and shall hiss him out of his place."*

The meaning of the word "hiss" in the Webster's Dictionary is "to make a sound like that of a prolonged s, as of a goose or snake when provoked or alarmed, or of escaping steam, air, etc. to show dislike or disapproval by hissing." Sometimes the audience will drive or force a performer off the stage by hissing at him.

130

When we hiss at the devil, we are speaking in his language (the serpent's language), and we are literally driving him off the stage." It is time we stop admiring his tactics and "boo" him out of the way or hiss him off the stage.

In Hebrew the word for "hiss" is *sharaq* which means "to whistle or hiss (as a call or in scorn)."

When Does God Use Hissing In A Positive Way?

In Zechariah 10:8,9 we read, *"I will hiss for them, and gather them; for I have redeemed them: and they shall increase as they have increased. And I will sow them among the people: and they shall remember me in far countries; and they shall live with their children, and turn again."*

This is a wonderful promise to dispersed Israel in this generation. God says here that He is going to "whistle" for them to come back and live with their children in their land.

So we see that we can "hiss" in a positive way, such as to issue a command of hope and deliverance and we can hiss at the enemy and force him off the stage because we are tired of watching his performance.

In the scriptures we see that often hissing was accompanied by clapping and wagging (or shaking) the head.

Both Isaiah and Zechariah prophesied that the Lord will hiss unto His people and call them from the ends of the earth.

Isaiah 5:26, *"And he will lift up an ensign to the nations from far, and will hiss unto them from the end of the earth: and, behold, they shall come with speed swiftly."*

This scripture goes on to describe the people that will hear the summons through the Lord's "whistle" and it is not an ordinary people. It is a description of the end-time army of the Lord *"Whose arrows are sharp, and all their bows bent, their horses' hoofs shall be counted like flint, and their wheels like a whirlwind: Their roaring shall be like a lion...."* (Isaiah 5:28,29) Read it through to the end of the chapter and you will see a description of a people who are much like Joel's end-time army. I believe that they will rise up from the ends of the earth at the same time as when the Jews return en masse to their land. This glorious day is about to happen really soon.

This end-time army that God is raising up knows the power of clapping, hissing, marching, laughing, shouting, praising, singing, and the uplifted hands. This army is efficiently trained for warfare. They are the Holy Ghost "Green Berets," and the French "Legion of Honour." They shall know their God and they shall be strong and do great exploits.

STUDY QUESTIONS

1. Memorize Job 27:23.

2. Why do we have power over the devil by hissing at him?

3. How can we "hiss" in a positive way?

CHAPTER ELEVEN

VICTORY THROUGH KEEPING SILENCE

There is a time when silence is the best battle-plan. Ecclesiastes 3:7 says, *"...a time to keep silence, and a time to speak."*

I believe that there are times in our lives when God seals up our mouths and does not let us say a single word.

Silent In Evil Times

Amos 5:13 warns us that in the days of wickedness one should keep quiet. *"Therefore the prudent shall keep silence in that time; for it is an evil time."* In Communist lands and countries that are under the control of despotic dictators, the people have grown wise to the prudence of silence.

Silent Before Fools

Proverbs 23:9, *"Speak not in the ears of a fool: for he will despise the wisdom of thy words."* We are fools if we share our hearts with fools.

Proverbs 26:4, *"Answer not a fool according to his folly."* Sometimes the best answer is the silent one.

The word "fool" comes from the Hebrew word *keciyl* (kes-eel), "to be fat, silly, foolish."

Snared By The Words Of Our Mouth And Condemned By The Words Of Our Mouth

Proverbs 6:2, *"Thou art snared with the words of thy mouth, thou art taken with the words of thy mouth."* The words that we have spoken can destroy us before they destroy the one about or against whom we spoke. On the day of judgment we will be judged by the words that we have spoken. Matthew 12:36,37, *"But I say unto you, That every idle word that men shall speak, they shall give account thereof in the day of judgment. For by thy words thou shalt be justified, and by thy words thou shalt be condemned."*

Proverbs 13:3, *"He that keepeth his mouth keepeth his life: but he that openeth wide his lips shall have destruction."*

"...if thou hast thought evil, lay thine hand upon thy mouth." (Proverbs 30:32) There is time we need to truly "think before we speak." May God help us to keep a "vow of silence" more often than we do!

Someone has said, "I am the master of my unspoken words, and the slave to those words that should have remained unsaid."

Examples Of Silence In The Bible

Joseph before his brethren: (Genesis 42-44) Joseph knew it was wise to hide his identity from his brothers until he could prove their sincerity. So he kept silent about who he was. Only when he had tried them and tested them, could he identify himself.

Sometimes God wants us to keep His secrets for only a while. But keeping God's secrets is another complete subject which I do not want to discuss now. I have taught on it and there are two tapes available on this subject which have been a blessing to many.*

---

*The tape TG134 "Keeping God's Secrets" by Gwen Shaw is available from End-Time Handmaidens

134

The Israelites when marching around Jericho: Joshua 6:10, *"And Joshua had commanded the people, saying, Ye shall not shout, nor make any noise with your voice, neither shall any word proceed out of your mouth, until the day I bid you shout; then shall ye shout."*

As we have already mentioned under the chapter on shouting, we have observed that one of the things that God commanded His people to do when marching around the city was that they must be absolutely silent. God knew that the people of Jericho would taunt them with mockery and criticism and God did not want His children to get involved with any secular conversation. I believe that God wants us to keep from getting involved with discussions that only gender strife.

Every one of us has to march around our own particular "Jericho" and we must ask the Lord to give us the strength to be silent until He bids us to speak and when we do, the "walls" of hindrance will fall down before us.

When Job was visited by his friends: *"So they sat down with him upon the ground seven days and seven nights, and none spake a word unto him: for they saw that his grief was very great."* (Job 2:13)

When someone is in great grief, a lot of words and idle talk will only add to their agony. It is enough to sit beside the one who is suffering, hold that one's hand and share their tears. A short prayer, a comforting card, a few flowers, a word anointed by the Holy Spirit will go a long way to assuage the grief of someone who has gone through deep trials. Many times they cannot speak about it and would prefer that you did not try to engage them in conversation that is only to satisfy your own curiosity. There are certain questions that God forbids us to ask people.

Jesus Christ was silent: a. Before the high priest:

135

Matthew 26:62, *"And the high priest arose, and said unto him, Answerest thou nothing? what is it which these witness against thee? But Jesus held his peace. And the high priest answered and said unto him, I adjure thee by the living God, that thou tell us whether thou be the Christ, the Son of God."*

The only reason that Jesus finally spoke up and answered the high priest was because he said to Him, "I adjure thee by the living God." The Lord was forced to answer him then.

b. **Before Pilate:** Matthew 27:14, *"And he answered him to never a word; insomuch that the governor marvelled greatly."* Jesus did not seek to defend Himself in any way or to save His life.

c. **Before Herod:** Luke 23:9, *"Then he questioned with him in many words; but he answered him nothing."* Jesus rose above Herod when He refused to answer him.

d. **In the presence of a sinner's accusers:** John 8:6, *"This they said, tempting him, that they might have to accuse him. But Jesus stooped down, and with his finger wrote on the ground, as though he heard them not."*

Jesus commanded His disciples to be silent concerning certain things: a. **The leper who was cleansed:** Matthew 8:4, *"And Jesus saith unto him, See thou tell no man...."* This was a command to the man whom He had just healed of leprosy.

b. **The blind men He healed:** Matthew 9:30, *"...and Jesus straitly charged them, saying, See that no man know it."*

c. **After great healing miracles:** *"And charged them that they should not make him known."* (Matthew 12:16)

d. **After the transfiguration:** *"...Jesus charged them, saying, Tell the vision to no man, until the Son of man be risen again from the dead."* (Matthew 17:9) There is sometimes a time factor as to when a secret can be revealed, but until then we must be careful to keep silent. There are other scriptures and incidents in the life of Christ just like these.

God said to Moses: Exodus 14:14, *"The Lord shall fight for you, and ye shall hold your peace* (you shall be silent). *"* When we are silent, the Lord can truly fight for us.

Elisha told the school of the prophets to be silent concerning Elijah's imminent translation: *"...Knowest thou that the Lord will take away thy master from thy head to day? And he said, Yea, I know it; hold ye your peace."* (II Kings 2:3)

God told Job to be silent: Job 33:31, *"Mark well, O Job, hearken unto me: hold thy peace, and I will speak."* Can you take this as a word from the Lord for your particular trial and testing? Believe God, that when He speaks, your adversary will hear every word that He has to say to him.

Proverbs 17:27 says, *"He that hath knowledge spareth his words...."*

In closing, let us remember the words of Jesus, *"But let your communication be, Yea, yea; Nay, nay: for whatsoever is more than these cometh of evil."* (Matthew 5:37)

There have been times in my life when God has literally sealed up my mouth and I was unable to say a single word. I couldn't talk. I could not even say, "Yea or nay." I know it was the protection of the Lord. Had I spoken, I might have said things that would have caused the other person to sympathize with me and it would have put me into a situation of compromise which God would not allow. God has always taken me the hard way. He has never permitted me to vindicate myself or prove another to be wrong. I must be careful that I do not transgress in what He permits in my life. I know that the day will come when God will speak openly on my behalf. I can wait that long.

Beloved, are you standing before your accusers? Answer them with silence. They cannot argue with silence. An argument needs an audible response. Let God be your voice of authority. Listen to Him say to you today, "Hold thy peace, and I will speak!"

Satan Is Not Omniscient

Many people think that the devil can read our thoughts. That would make him equal with God. I do not believe that God has given him this power. But he has a lot of "demon-spies" who are active in listening in and hearing what we say. He also has the power to suggest things to our minds. Therefore when we voice our opinions, and they are negative, Satan knows how to attack us. He eavesdrops on every conversation and also our prayers. God has given us the gift of praying in tongues. We need to use this prayer language because it is only understood by the Holy Spirit. We do not pray in tongues as much as we ought to. If we realized the power that it is, we would always pray in the heavenly language when we are in intercession alone with the Lord.

I don't believe we will ever forget the courageous and magnificent rescue of the hijacked hostages that Israel made at Entebbe airport, Uganda, during the regime of Idi Amin. The key to their great success was their complete secrecy. Without secrecy, our armies are defeated before they march. This was also the key to the great victory America so recently won in their raid on Grenada. The world screamed and the media abused, but we accomplished our purpose and hundreds of lives were saved, as well as a whole island.

We are in warfare. We are not in a campaign to make friends. Jesus said, *"Think not that I am come to send peace on earth: I came not to send peace, but a sword."* (Matthew 10:34) Remember, don't give the devil any information which he can use against you or against those you love.

STUDY QUESTIONS

1. Read Genesis 42-44.

2. Memorize Proverbs 13:3.

3. Mention two cases in which we should be silent.

4. Why did the children of Israel have to be silent when they marched around Jericho?

5. Why do you think Jesus remained silent before His accusers?

Jeremiah in the Court of the Prison Buying His Kinsman's Field

CHAPTER TWELVE

VICTORY THROUGH THE "DOCUMENT
OF CONFIRMATION"

This is one of the most neglected and powerful weapons of spiritual warfare that all of us possess but few of us use. Let us get the scriptural basis for it.

God Commands Ezekiel To Write A Document Of War

In Ezekiel 24:1,2 we read, *"Again in the ninth year, in the tenth month, in the tenth day of the month, the word of the Lord came unto me, saying, Son of man, write thee the name of the day, even of this same day: the king of Babylon set himself against Jerusalem this same day."*
In those days there was no means of instant communication like there is now. The secrets of Nebuchadnezzar's heart were probably not even revealed to his own military officers. Only in his heart came the determination to launch an all-out attack against Jerusalem. But God, who knows the secrets of all hearts, and who has the best espionage system, told His prophet what had taken place in the heart of a king who was far distant from Jerusalem. God also told him to mark the date down, so that he would know later that that which God had told him was the truth.
There are times when God tells you something in your heart, but you do not write it down. Later you forget all about it. Or perhaps Satan takes these truths away from you and you begin to have doubts about them. But when you have once "recorded" the word of the Lord to you, you have something to look back on, sometimes years later, to confirm the Word that God spoke to you.

141

The written word is very important to God. He holds it in high esteem. He will always stand behind it to bring it to pass and fulfil every "jot and tittle." (Matthew 5:18) The words "it is written" are recorded many times in the Bible. This shows us how great an importance God places upon that which has been recorded in His name.

Perhaps one of the keys to the power and authority of writing down that which God speaks to you is found in Daniel 6:8, *"Now, O king, establish the decree, and sign the writing, that it be not changed...."* The written laws or decrees of the Mede and Persian Empire could not be changed. How much more will God stand behind His Word to fulfil it and bring all to pass which He has promised!

God Commanded Moses To Document His Words To Israel

Exodus 34:27, *"And the Lord said unto Moses, Write thou these words: for after the tenor of these words I have made a covenant with thee and with Israel."*

The word which God had written on the tables, when Moses first went up the Mount of Sinai to speak with God, were so important that when Moses broke the tablets, God immediately re-wrote these words again for him the second time. If it was not important to have them in writing, then the Lord would not have written them out. He wrote it with His own finger, thus making us realize the great importance of the written and sealed document of the covenant which God made with Israel.

A document is described in Webster's Dictionary as "a lesson, a proof, anything printed, written, relied upon to record or prove something. Anything serving as proof, to prove or support, as by reference to documents."

God speaks many things to His children, but because

we are forgetful we cannot remember the things and the many times He has spoken to us. Therefore it is good to record the Word of the Lord to us. It is good to record personal prophecies which we have received under the anointing of the Holy Spirit. The prophecies which God has given in the Bible to certain people were recorded and we can read how they were fulfilled. For example,

1. Samuel's prophecy to Saul (I Samuel 10:5-11)
2. Samuel's prophecy to David (I Samuel 16:13)
3. A prophet's prophecy to Jeroboam (I Kings 13:1-6)
4. Ahijah's prophecy to Jeroboam (I Kings 11:30,31)
5. Elijah's prophecy to Ahab (I Kings 21:19; I Kings 22:38)
6. Jesus' prophecy to Peter (John 21:18,19)
7. Agabus' prophecy to Paul (Acts 21:11).

There are many others. They were recorded for us to read and to understand the ways of God's dealings with His people and the authority of His Word.

Isaiah's Record About Cyrus

One of the most amazing recorded promises that God ever made was about Cyrus. (Isaiah 44:28-45:3) He foretells the name of a man who shall do all His will and who shall rebuild the temple in Jerusalem 100 years before it was even destroyed. I love this scripture. It gives me such strong faith. I see how God knows my future, my name and my whole life's calling long before I ever was born, even from the foundation of the world. And what is so beautiful is that by this scripture we realize that God has a heavenly blue-print for every life, just like He had it for

143

Cyrus. After our work is finished, and we are permitted to see our blue-print in heaven, I pray that we will not have digressed even one iota from that which the Lord planned for us.

Daniel Knew God's Plan Because Of The Records God Gave Through His Prophets

In Daniel 10:1 we read, *"In the third year of Cyrus king of Persia a thing was revealed unto Daniel, whose name was called Belteshazzar; and the thing was true, but the time appointed was long: and he understood the thing, and had understanding of the vision."*

Daniel knew that the time had come for his people to return to Jerusalem because he had the record of the prophetic promise which God had commanded Jeremiah (Jeremiah 25:11) and Isaiah (Isaiah 44:28-45:4) to record. God had even given the length of years that they would be in captivity (70) and the name of the man (Cyrus) who would rebuild Jerusalem. This written word gave Daniel the strength to fast and seek God for a miracle to take place that would release his people. When we have "the word of the Lord" to us, it strengthens us.

Prophecies In My Life

Before I went to Taiwan, as a second-term missionary in 1951, a mighty prophecy was given over me in a very anointed farewell meeting. Someone in the audience wrote down that prophecy and gave it to me. I kept it through my years of service to God on the missionary field and it was often a great source of strength to me.

Later, different prophecies have been given to me which

144

came in times of testing or before entering a new door, or during times of great responsibilities and these "words of the Lord" to me have always been a great source of strength and encouragement to me. I would never have been able to remember them as they were given, but someone wrote them down, or they were recorded and so I had this "document of God's covenant relationship with me" to refer to again and again when I needed it.

God is speaking in these days in a powerful, new way through His prophets. He is speaking also in dreams and visions. We often include them in our letters and our news bulletin, because we place much importance on what God is saying. Prophecies that are truly from the Lord need to be heeded. It is also important to judge (I Corinthians 14:29) whether prophecies are truly from the Lord. Deuteronomy 13:1-3 and 18:22 tell us a prophecy which does not come to pass or one which leads people to follow other gods is not from God. The "prophet" has spoken presumptiously or is a false prophet and should not be heeded nor feared.

Covenant Renewed In Writing

When God's people returned from captivity to Jerusalem, Nehemiah commanded them to renew their covenant relationship with God. Nehemiah 9:38, *"And because of all this we make a sure covenant, and write it; and our princes, Levites, and priests, seal unto it."*

The Covenant Of The Pilgrim Fathers

Every American remembers the covenant that was written by our forefathers who landed on the Mayflower. This covenant, usually called the "Mayflower Compact" was signed by 41 men on November 21, 1620. It was a covenant of loyalty to God and to each other. As long as they lived by this covenant, God blessed the pilgrims. Those godly people had a vision from the Lord and for this blessed land and God has been faithful to keep His part of the covenant which they made. The tragedy is that we have not been faithful to keep our part of the covenant. God will hold us responsible for this.

God Commanded Habbakuk To Record The Vision

Habakkuk 2:2,3, *"And the Lord answered me, and said, Write the vision, and make it plain upon tables, that he may run that readeth it. For the vision is yet for an appointed time, but at the end it shall speak, and not lie: though it tarry, wait for it; because it will surely come, it will not tarry."* The Living Bible says, "They will not be overdue a single day."

God commanded Habbakuk, His prophet, to record the vision which He had given to him. He said that it would be a witness in the end-time. When God speaks to you, you may forget what He has spoken, but if you record it, you and your children and your children's children will have proof of God's covenant relationship with you.

God has respect for the written and signed document.

God Made A Covenant With Israel Which He Commanded To Be Recorded

Psalm 102:18, *"This shall be written for the generation to come: and the people which shall be created shall praise the Lord."* The recording of the word of the Lord to you, sometimes is for others as much as it is for yourself. God

146

told His people that the "generation to come" would read
the covenant which God had made with Israel and it would
bring praises to His name. Translating from the original
Hebrew the words "the generation to come" say "the last
generation."

Jeremiah Is Commanded By God To Write
An Evidence Of Purchase (Jeremiah 32:6-26)

Jeremiah was in prison when the Lord told him that his
cousin would come to him and ask him to buy his field in
Anathoth. God told him that He wanted Jeremiah to
accept this offer. When his cousin came and made the offer,
Jeremiah accepted it because he knew it was the word of
the Lord. He paid him 17 shekels of silver and *"...subscribed
the evidence, and sealed it, and took witnesses, and weighed
him the money in the balances."* (Verse 10) He gave this
evidence of the purchase to Baruch in the presence of his
relative and other witnesses that were in the prison. He told
Baruch to take this "evidence of purchase" and place it in
an earthen vessel where it would be sure to last a long time.
(We know from the recently discovered Dead Sea scrolls
that documents placed in earthen jars have kept 2,000 years
and longer). He made the bold declaration, *"Thus saith the
Lord of hosts, the God of Israel; Houses and fields and
vineyards shall be possessed again in this land."* And he
made this statement on the eve of their being carried into
captivity when all land was practically unsaleable and
worthless. But he believed God in the face of all the wrath
and judgment of God that was soon to fall upon them.
Jeremiah said, *"Behold the mounts* [siege mounds], *they are
come unto the city to take it; and the city is given unto the
hand of the Chaldeans, that fight against it, because of the*

147

sword, and of the famine, and of the pestilence: and what thou hast spoken is come to pass; and, behold, thou seest it. And thou hast said unto me, O Lord God, Buy thee the field for money, and take witnesses; for the city is given into the hand of the Chaldeans." (Verses 24,25) Then, he goes on to prophesy how Jerusalem would fall to Nebuchadnezzar, king of Babylon, who would destroy it with fire, burn all its houses where they had worshipped idols from the roof-tops, and carry the people into captivity, but in the end God would *"...gather them out of all countries...and I will bring them again unto this place, and I will cause them to dwell safely:...And I will make an everlasting covenant with them....."* (Jeremiah 32:37,40)

Then He said, *"And fields shall be bought in this land, whereof ye say, It is desolate without man or beast; it is given into the hand of the Chaldeans. Men shall buy fields for money, and subscribe evidences, and seal them, and take witnesses in the land of Benjamin, and in the places about Jerusalem, and in the cities of Judah, and in the cities of the mountains, and in the cities of the valley, and in the cities of the south: for I will cause their captivity to return, saith the Lord."* (Jeremiah 32:43,44)

Jeremiah was forced to go into Egypt with the remnant that remained after the people were carried away captive and there is no record that he ever returned. But somewhere in the field of Anathoth there is an earthen jar today that has the record of the evidence of purchase which Jeremiah made with his cousin, Hanameel. Of course, it could have been put somewhere else but I believe that that is where it was kept. God has fulfilled all His word to Jeremiah. The children of Judah did return and land was again bought and sold. Today, land in Jerusalem is the most precious and highest priced of any place on earth. Surely

God is faithful!

Has He spoken to you? Do not doubt His pomises to you! Write it down. Later, when you read that which He has spoken, it will bring blessing to your life, and long after you are gone, others, another generation, shall also be blessed and praise the Lord. Remember, though the vision tarry, wait for it; because it will surely come to pass.

When God gives you a promise in His Word, claim it and put the date beside it. Years later you will be blessed at remembering how God gave you that miracle which He promised you.

STUDY QUESTIONS

1. Read Jeremiah 32.

2. Memorize Habakkuk 2:3.

3. Why is it important to write down what God tells you?

4. Mention five prophecies that were recorded in the Bible.

5. Did you ever receive a word from God, record it and hold on to it until it came to pass?

CHAPTER THIRTEEN

VICTORY THROUGH PRAYING IN TONGUES

Praying in tongues — or praying in the Spirit — is one of the most effectual ways of obtaining the victory over all demonic warfare that God has made available. Yet it has been the most maligned, ridiculed and fought against by an unbelieving church of the gifts of the Holy Spirit.

Why Satan Hates Tongues

Perhaps the reason that Satan has attacked speaking and praying in tongues more than any of the other gifts of the Holy Spirit is because he knows that when the whole church of Jesus Christ, universal, enters into the power of intercessory prayer through praying in the power of the Holy Ghost, his power will be lost. Satan does not war against tongues for nothing. He will permit and even promote all kinds of religious activities and programming because he wants to keep us so busy running about, entertaining and being entertained that we have no time to attack his kingdom through praying in the Holy Ghost. The last thing that Satan wants is for us to tear down his strongholds. He knows that the power of the Holy Ghost will aim directly and effectually right where he is most vulnerable, and that is in the things that concern the spiritual realm. So he tries to keep us in the carnal realm. For once we rise into the warfare by the Holy Spirit, we will be more than conquerors through Jesus Christ who loved us and gave Himself for us.

Tongues Always Accompany New Revival

Every great outpouring of the Holy Spirit, since the

days of Pentecost, was accompanied by much praying in tongues. It was the phenomenon of tongues that accompanied the outpouring of the Holy Spirit in Azusa Street and many other places in America during the turn of this century that shook the world. God clearly shows the virtue of speaking in tongues by making it the prime manifestation which accompanies the infilling of the Holy Spirit.

The Difference Between Speaking In Tongues And Praying In Tongues

Speaking in tongues and praying in tongues is one gift with two different ministries. Speaking in tongues is a gift to be used to worship and praise the Lord and to exhort the church. When it is used by the Holy Spirit for the edification of the church it must be accompanied by the gift of interpretation of tongues. (I Corinthians 14:5)

"He that speaketh in an unknown tongue edifieth himself...." (I Corinthians 14:4) God has given us a way in which we can be built up, encouraged and strengthened in the Spirit, and that way is by speaking in tongues. But this is mostly for private worship, except it be interpreted for the body.

Paul said, *"I thank my God, I speak with tongues more than ye all:"* (I Corinthians 14:18) Paul honoured the gift of the language of the Holy Spirit. When you speak and pray in tongues, you are allowing the Holy Spirit to communicate with God, the Father, using your body as the holy tabernacle where the high priest, Jesus, Himself resides. You become the very place where the Shekinah of glory dwells.

In the early days of the outpouring of the Holy Spirit in the United States, many were slain in the Spirit before they

151

were filled with the Holy Spirit. They broke out, speaking in other tongues.

God does not want us to hasten away from the place of His dealings with us. We are so quick to "pick people up" off the floor when they are slain by the Spirit. But in the earlier days we often laid there for hours while God's Spirit did some real spiritual and physical surgery in our lives. Oh, how we need to return to that pattern!

Praying In The Spirit

Paul said, *"For if I pray in an unknown tongue, my spirit prayeth...."* (I Corinthians 14:14)

God has given us an easy way to live a life of prayer. Our spirits can pray without our minds thinking of every word we speak. People who are not gifted in oratory or who are slow of speech can enter a new life of prayer without any feelings of inferiority, by letting the Holy Spirit pray through them! Some quiet people become the world's greatest intercessors when they allow the Spirit of God to pray through their spirit. This is the rest which the Holy Spirit promised in Isaiah 28:11,12, *"For with stammering lips and another tongue will he speak to this people. To whom he said, This is the rest wherewith ye may cause the weary to rest; and this is the refreshing...."*

When we are praying and worshipping in tongues privately, we are putting a guard of protection over our minds, our bodies, our souls and our spirits. Demon spirits hate praying in tongues more than any other form of prayer. They always back off.

Tommy's Vision

I will always remember how God taught us the power of praying in tongues.

My father and I raised a tent for evangelistic meetings in Ontario. We had much opposition from the local churches. The enemy always fights saints through "saints."

The night that we started these meetings, we could feel the warfare. Even some who had been close to us were avoiding us because they didn't want to be identified with us.

After preaching, I gave the altar call, and the elders and others who had come up to "spy out the camp" came forward. As I prayed with them, they were all slain in the Spirit, and began to travail and praise and worship as the Holy Ghost fell on the people.

My youngest son, Tommy, was also praying at the altar. In those days he was my "number one" intercessor. He would travail for hours in the Spirit, even though he was only ten years old. That night he was in unusual deep travail. So much so, that it almost frightened me. I repeatedly left the people with whom I was praying and went over to pray with him. When the burden of travail got heavy, he would just agonize in the heavenly prayer language. It seemed to come over him in waves.

After the burden lifted, he told us how he was in the very "dungeons of hell" and the demon spirits would attack him. Every time he cried out in tongues, they would fall back. This happened over and over again that night. Tommy saw the demons literally attacking the ministry, but when he cried out, each time praying in tongues, they were forced to flee. They hated his praying in tongues.

God has given us the prayer of the Spirit for high war-

153

fare. These are dark days. There will be more and more demonic attacks against the anointed ministries. God has provided all the armour you need.

Praying And Singing In The Spirit

Praying in the Spirit should not replace praying with the understanding. Both have their place.

We read, *"...I will pray with the spirit, and I will pray with the understanding also: I will sing with the spirit, and I will sing with the understanding also."* (I Corinthians 14:15)

There is a song in the Spirit which is so edifying, uplifting and worshipful that it lifts us up into the heavens. When a whole church sings in the Spirit, it is so much like the music of heaven that in the old days they called it the "heavenly choir."

We need to sing in the Spirit as much as we need to pray in the Spirit. Heaven dips low when we sing in the Spirit.

Why Is Praying In The Spirit Powerful?

1. **When we pray in the Spirit we pray in the will of God.**

The Apostle James said, *"Ye ask, and receive not, because ye ask amiss, that ye may consume it upon your lusts."* (James 4:3)

Many times we ask God for the wrong things. We pray for things that are not the will of God. This kind of praying is never going to be answered. Sometimes we may not intentionally pray against the will of God, we may be doing it in ignorance. But when we pray with the understanding, we pray with limited vision and limited wisdom.

154

When we pray in the Spirit, we always pray the will of God. When we pray the will of God, our prayers are answered. I John 5:14,15 says, *"And this is the confidence that we have in him, that, if we ask any thing according to his will, he heareth us: And if we know that he hear us, whatsoever we ask, we know that we have the petitions that we desired of him."*

Anything we ask in His will is answered. But how can we always know His will?

A woman phones me and asks me to pray about her marriage. She tells me her husband has a violent temper, beats her and abuses her. He also has a demon of lust and a 5-year-old daughter has been physically molested by his demons of incest. How do I pray? Do I ask God to give her strength to live with him and subject little Annie to more violence and perversion? Do I pray for her to have the grace to leave him? She wants to know what she should do. She has prayed for him for a long time, but there has been no change in him. He has only grown worse.

I know that the Holy Ghost knows what God's will is, He knows what has happened in the past. He also knows what can happen in the future, and so He knows how to pray. Therefore, I must pray in the Spirit. The Holy Spirit's prayer is always the right prayer.

The Holy Spirit has been given to us to help us pray prayers that will be answered because they are prayed according to God's will.

2. **When we pray in the Spirit, we are not praying in unbelief.**

The Holy Spirit has perfect faith in the Father. When He prays through us, the prayer is not mixed with unbelief.

I John 3:21,22 says, *"Beloved, if our heart condemn us not, then have we confidence toward God. And whatso-*

ever we ask, we receive of him, because we keep his commandments, and do those things that are pleasing in his sight."

The Holy Spirit is pure and faultless. God will always hear His prayers and answer them. When I pray, I know very well my imperfections and my weaknesses. The devil says, "Who do you think you are? How can God answer your prayers when you are so faulty?"

But praise God, Satan cannot accuse the Holy Spirit of being faulty. Therefore the prayer of the Spirit is always filled with faith and confidence. That is why the prayers of many are answered even when we know their lives are not what they should be.

I am not saying we should live in sin and still have the Holy Spirit pray through us. For we must strive in all ways to live in holiness and obedience to His highest will. But I want you to understand that when the Spirit of God prays through you, His prayer is a prayer of faith and confidence. He knows that whatsoever He asks of God, the Father, He will receive from Him.

The Spirit Prays For Forgiveness

The Holy Spirit's prayer does a work of cleansing in our lives. I remember when I was preaching in Hong Kong and the Spirit was poured out. I heard a Chinese woman who could not speak a single word of English praying in perfect English. She kept saying the same thing over and over again, "Oh God, forgive my great sin; O God forgive my great sin."

I wondered if she could maybe understand English, but when I tried to converse with her, she couldn't speak or understand a word of what I said.

Upon inquiring, I found that she had been going with her son to the horse races and they had been gambling, trying to make some fast money. This had grieved the Holy Spirit. God hates gambling. The Holy Spirit had been interceding for this woman before the Lord.

The Holy Spirit Intercedes For The Church

When we were in Pakistan, we attended a Christmas church meeting. I was suddenly very surprised to hear a young Pakistani man pray in perfect American English. This is what alerted me. Usually, in that part of the world, the natives who speak English, speak with a British accent because they have been under the influence of the British so long. But this young man did not have a British accent.

But most soul-stirring of all was the prayer which the Holy Spirit prayed through him.

Here it is, "Where is the church? Where is the church? It is so faulty. It's coming short. Where's it going? Where's it going? So many churches...Where is the salt? It's not His fault. No, No, it's the church's fault."

The Holy Spirit was travailing for the backslidden church of Pakistan and the whole world.

3. **Praying in the Spirit breaks through our limitations.**

Last of all, I want to draw your attention to the powerful scripture in Romans 8:26-28, *"Likewise the Spirit also helpeth our infirmities: for we know not what we should pray for as we ought: but the Spirit itself maketh intercession for us with groanings which cannot be uttered. And he that searcheth the hearts knoweth what is the mind of the Spirit, because he maketh intercession for the saints according to the will of God. And we know that all things work together for good to them that love God, to them who*

157

are the called according to his purpose."

The Spirit of God knows our infirmities, weaknesses and our limitations, and He has been given to us to help us. We do not know how to pray or what to pray, so He Himself uses our tongues, bypassing our understanding and makes intercession for us. He is the one who knows what is in every heart of man. He also knows the heart of God. It is His work to line up the heart of man which is so prone to go astray with the heart of God. When we pray in the Spirit, we are not only bringing ourselves in line with God's will, He is also praying through us for all saints to be brought into God's divine plan for their lives. And I am sure the Holy Spirit is also travailing and interceding for souls who are unsaved, the multitudes of lost around the world.

Does the conduct of one of God's children grieve you? Does the coldness or lukewarmness of the church grieve you? Does the sin of worldliness of those who call themselves Christians break your heart? Are you living in a situation which you cannot change? Are you burdened, heart-broken and weary? Then, let the Holy Spirit pray through you. Pray, pray, pray without ceasing.

Do you sometimes wonder at how people who are not living what you would consider a consistent Christian life, are still able to pray in tongues? And have you wondered why this is so? I would like to tell you that it is the Holy Spirit praying through them, interceding on their behalf.

I remember an incident that happened in Inner Mongolia. One of the elders of the church backslid. He was living in adultery. But nobody knew about it. One day during prayer time at the church, he began to pray in what to him was an unknown tongue, but to the missionaries from Sweden it was very well-known, for he was praying in the

158

Swedish language. The Holy Spirit was travailing through him, confessing his sin of adultery, and pleading for God to be merciful and to deliver him from the clutches of the devil.

The missionaries were shocked when they heard the Spirit praying through this elder. They did not even know he had fallen into sin. When they confronted him with it, he broke down and confessed his sin to them.

This shows us that when we pray in tongues, the Holy Spirit could be interceding even for ourselves.

Pray while working, pray while sitting in church. Wherever you are, at all times you can pray in the Spirit.

When someone has hurt you deeply, broken your heart, and cast you aside, you may find it impossible to pray for that one with the understanding. It hurts too much to even think about it. You aren't even sure if you can forgive that one. So how can you pray for them? I would like to encourage you to pray for him or her in the Spirit. It is the only way you can pray a pure prayer for that one who has offended and grieved you deeply.

Paul, the great intercessor admonishes us, *"Praying always with all prayer and supplication in the Spirit, and watching thereunto with all perseverance and supplication for all saints."* (Ephesians 6:18)

The only way we can live a life of prayer is by praying in the Spirit. Pray in tongues and let God do mighty things through your life.

STUDY QUESTIONS

1. Read I Corinthians 14.

2. Memorize Romans 8:24-26.

3. Why does Satan hate the gift of tongues so much?

4. What is the difference between praying in tongues and speaking in tongues?

5. How can we pray the perfect will of God and with complete faith?

CHAPTER FOURTEEN

VICTORY THROUGH TITHING

One of the biggest hindrances to answered prayer lies not with the devil and his demons, but our own greedy, selfish selves.

The key to prosperity, blessings and good health still lies with obeying God's law of giving our tithes and offerings to the Lord. The Word of God is very clear about it.

There have been times when I have not been permitted by the Holy Spirit to pray for God to meet the needs of certain persons because they were not tithing.

The blessing of God comes upon our lives through the law of giving. There is no way that we can get around it. As we give, God gives to us.

Proverbs 3:9,10 says very clearly, *"Honour the Lord with thy substance, and with the firstfruits of all thine increase: So shall thy barns be filled with plenty, and thy presses shall burst out with new wine."*

This is the key to God's provision and also to His overflow. It is the law of sowing and reaping.

The truth of tithing is seen all through the Bible.

Abraham Tithed

In Genesis 14:20 we read that when Abraham met Melchizedek as he returned from the battle, he gave Melchizedek tithes of all. Melchizedek, who was the priest of the Most High God, received these tithes and blessed Abraham. He said, *"...Blessed be Abram of the most high God, possessor of heaven and earth: And blessed be the most high God, which hath delivered thine enemies into thy hand."* (Genesis 14:19,20)

When Abraham gave tithes to Melchizedek, it was a proof that the giving of tithes was not only a law to be observed under the Mosaic Law of the old covenant, as some would like us to believe, but an eternal law of blessing.

God gave us this testimony to show us the blessing that lies in giving to those who are priests of the Most High God.

Hebrews 7:5, *"And verily they that are of the sons of Levi, who receive the office of the priesthood, have a commandment to take tithes of the people according to the law, that is, of their brethren, though they come out of the loins of Abraham."* This scripture clarifies that those who served God in the Levitical priesthood were commanded to receive tithes. Sometimes it is harder to receive than to give.

The writer of Hebrews is saying here that though the Levites were the descendants of Abraham (who had given tithes), God had ordained that they should now be the recipients of the tithes.

Hebrews 7:6, *"But he whose descent is not counted from them received tithes of Abraham, and blessed him that had the promises."* The writer says that the one who received tithes from Abraham was not of the Levitical family. In fact, there is no family connection at all between Melchizedek and Israel. The genealogy of Melchizedek is a mystery.

Hebrews 7:8, *"And here men that die receive tithes; but there he receiveth them, of whom it is witnessed that he liveth."* This gives us the hint that Melchizedek was "he of whom it is witnessed that he liveth." Could this Melchizedek have been the pre-incarnate Christ? Many Bible scholars believe that he was.

Hebrews 7:9, *"And as I may so say, Levi also, who*

162

receiveth tithes, payed tithes in Abraham." This scripture says that Levi, in a sense, paid tithes too, for he was then in the loins of Abraham. We bring God's blessing upon those children who are still "in the loins." Many times we see how those who have given generously to God bring a blessing upon their family unto the third and fourth generation.

Jacob Tithed

In Genesis 28:22 we read Jacob's vow to God, *"...of all that thou shalt give me I will surely give the tenth unto thee."*

Jacob was blessed in a supernatural way financially. God gave him the key of how to get wealth. We read that even Laban, his father-in-law, recognized the blessing of God upon Jacob. *"And Laban said unto him, I pray thee, if I have found favour in thine eyes, tarry: for I have learned by experience that the Lord hath blessed me for thy sake."* (Genesis 30:27) Laban had to see that the blessing of God was upon Jacob in a sovereign way. Yet he did not ask Jacob the reason for his blessed life. Instead, after a while, he became full of envy. Many become jealous of those whom God is blessing when all they need to do is to begin to pay their tithes and they will be blessed, too, for God is no respecter of persons.

Genesis 30:43 says, *"And the man (Jacob) increased exceedingly, and had much cattle, and maidservants, and menservants, and camels, and asses."*

God said to Jacob, *"I am the God of Bethel, where thou anointedst the pillar, and where thou vowedst a vow unto me...."* (Genesis 31:13) God never forgets the vow you make to Him, and if you will faithfully keep your side of

163

the vow, God will surely keep His. He cannot fail you.

God wants to bless us. But He is waiting for us to give, that we, ourselves, can open the windows of heaven. There are many great doors that are closed to God's people which only prayer and fasting can open, but the door to God's supply is not opened by prayer and fasting. It is opened by giving. That is the way God decreed it should be, and that is the way it is, and we cannot alter it, no matter how we try.

God Commanded Israel To Tithe

God told Israel that one tenth of all that they had belonged to Him, whether it was cattle or grain or whatever. The firstling of every beast, and of the field was the Lord's. (Leviticus 27:26)

If it was an unclean beast, such as an ass, it was to be redeemed and a substitute offering was to be given in its place. God said that the first-fruit of man and beast was "most holy unto the Lord."

"And all the tithe of the land, whether of the seed of the land, or of the fruit of the tree, is the Lord's: it is holy unto the Lord...And concerning the tithe of the herd, or of the flock....the tenth shall be holy unto the Lord. He shall not search whether it be good or bad, neither shall he change it:...These are the commandments, which the Lord commanded Moses for the children of Israel in mount Sinai." (Leviticus 27:30-34)

The tithes of Israel were for the priesthood. God told the tribe of Levi that they could have no tribal possessions. They would live off the tithes of the children of Israel. Israel was commanded to bring their tithes unto the priests. *"And the Lord spake unto Aaron, Thou shalt have no*

164

inheritance in their land, neither shalt thou have any part among them: I am thy part and thine inheritance among the children of Israel. And, behold, I have given the children of Levi all the tenth in Israel for an inheritance, for their service which they serve, even the service of the tabernacle of the congregation...But the **tithes** *of the children of Israel, which they offer as an heave offering unto the Lord, I have given to the Levites to inherit: therefore I have said unto them, Among the children of Israel they shall have no inheritance...Thus speak unto the Levites, and say unto them, When ye take of the children of Israel the* **tithes** *which I have given you from them for your inheritance, then ye shall offer up an heave offering of it for the Lord, even a tenth part of the* **tithe**... *Thus ye also shall offer an heave offering unto the Lord of all your* **tithes**, *which ye receive of the children of Israel; and ye shall give thereof the Lord's heave offering to Aaron the priest."* (Numbers 18:20,21,24,26,28)

The law of tithing affected everything Israel possessed. *"And to bring the firstfruits of our ground, and the first-fruits of all fruit of all trees, year by year, unto the house of the Lord: Also the firstborn of our sons, and of our cattle, as it is written in the law, and the firstlings of our herds and of our flocks, to bring to the house of our God, unto the priests that minister in the house of our God: And that we should bring the firstfruits of our dough, and our offerings, and the fruit of all manner of trees, of wine and of oil, unto the priests, to the chambers of the house of our God; and the tithes of our ground unto the Levites, that the same Levites might have the tithes in all the cities of our tillage."* (Nehemiah 10:35-37)

The Levites Tithed

Not only did the children of Israel tithe to the Levites throughout the land, the Levites were commanded to *"...bring up* **the tithe of the tithes** *unto the house of our God, to the chambers, into the treasure house...we will not forsake the house of our God."* (Nehemiah 10:38,39) This was the command of Nehemiah to God's people when they returned from the captivity.

Jesus Condoned Tithing

Jesus mentioned the fact that God's people tithe, and He did not speak against it nor command it to be stopped, but He did say that they must not omit the importance of true judgment, mercy and faith. He said, *"...judgment, mercy, and faith: these ought ye to have done, AND NOT TO LEAVE THE OTHER* (tithing) *UNDONE."* (Matthew 23:23) In other words, Jesus says, "Don't stop tithing!"

Have you "left undone" the giving of your tithes? God's blessing hangs like a glory cloud over your head, waiting for you to release it by pouring out from your meagre supply. Give and give and give again. Don't only give to one ministry or one nation, give to many. Sow your seed in many fields. The Word of God says very clearly, *"Give a portion to seven, and also to eight....If the clouds be full of rain, they empty themselves upon the earth...."* (Ecclesiastes 11:2,3)

The Miracle Of Supply Comes When We "Pour Out"

When the widow of Israel was in desperate straits because she could not pay her debts and her creditor threatened

166

to take her two sons as bondslaves, she went to the prophet Elisha. He asked her, *"...what hast thou in the house?..."* (II Kings 4:2) She answered that all that she had was a pot of oil. He told her to go and borrow all the vessels she could get hold of ("...borrow not a few"), and bring them into her house, shut the door and "pour out." It was when she started to pour out that the law of God's miracle supply was released to her and the woman tapped into God's eternal oil well of golden cooking oil. I believe that was the best oil ever sold in Israel!

God can do the same today. God will meet your need. He will save your children, pay your debts and even give you a secure "pension" for your old age if you will begin to pour out. Don't ever limit God. That widow limited God when she brought in the last of the pots. Every pot she brought in was filled. You put the limits on God.

The Early Church Gave To God's Work

After God poured out His Spirit upon the early church, the ministry was supported by the generosity of the saints. No more was it necessary for them to buy lambs and doves to offer as sacrifices in the temple because the sacrifice had been made by Jesus Christ. They also no longer supported the priests who were under the old order because the old order was done away with, with the ushering in of the New Covenant. So now they gave their tithes to the apostles and to the new missionary enterprises that God had started through the outpouring of the Holy Spirit on the early church. They not only brought their tithes and offerings to the early church, but they sold their possessions and brought their money and laid it at the apostles' feet. (Acts 4:34-37) No one lacked anything. This kind of generosity can only accompany a great revival or supernatural visitation of God in a person's life. We are all so prone to think that all we have is ours forever, but it is only loaned to us.

New Testament Missionary Vision Was Supported By The Donations Of God's People

Over and over again Paul mentions the generous giving of God's people. In II Corinthians 8:1-5 we read, *"Moreover, brethren, we do you to wit of the grace of God bestowed on the churches of Macedonia; How that in a great trial of affliction the abundance of their joy and their deep poverty abounded unto the riches of their liberality. For to their power, I bear record, yea, and beyond their power they were willing of themselves; Praying us with much intreaty that we would receive the gift, and take upon us the fellowship of the ministering to the saints. And this they did, not as we hoped, but first gave their own selves to the Lord, and unto us by the will of God."* Paul mentions the great joy that God's people had in giving. And truly they did. To give is always a joyful thing. The writer of Acts quotes Paul as saying to the elders of Ephesus, *"...remember the words of the Lord Jesus, how he said, It is more blessed to give than to receive."* (Acts 20:35)

God Loves A Cheerful Giver

The Lord loves to see us give hilariously. When people argue against giving God a tithe or an offering, it usually indicates a greedy and selfish spirit. All that we give to God is stored up for us in heaven.

My father used to say, "God is no man's debtor. If you

168

give to God, He will give to you."

As I already told you on page 10, when my parents began to tithe we were very poor. We had just moved from Sasketchewan to Ontario, Canada, and we had failed in a business venture. We were in a strange country without friends or relatives. But during this time my parents heard the true teachings of the Baptism of the Holy Ghost, and they were filled with the Holy Spirit and began to tithe. My father got a job as a farm manager. His wages were $35.00 a month. He had a wife and three children to support. Our house was big and draughty. It would need a lot of fuel to keep us warm all winter. Dad went out in the coal shed and looked at those few lumps of coal that were lying there, and he made a covenant with God to give God his tithes. It was only $3.50 a month, but it was a lot for him. The winter came — cold, damp and windy. We kept the heater burning day and night. My brother, Jamie, was born that winter, so we had to keep the house warm.

Finally, spring came! My dad went back to the coal shed to visit God again. There lay the coal! There was as much as there had been in the fall. God had miraculously kept up the supply. We had not bought one bag of coal all winter long. The same God who multiplied the loaves and the fishes, had multiplied the coal. From that day on, my father never stopped tithing, and God blessed him and restored all that he had lost and much more. Today the home which God gave him, is our missionary headquarters in Niagara Falls. New York, Rainbow House. The promise of God's provision is still on that house because it was laid on the foundation of giving to God.

How Much Shall We Give To God?

The children of Israel gave their tithes and their offerings and their first-fruits. You cannot outgive God. When you give, the angels report it in the account books of heaven and the Lord takes notice of it. A blessing is decreed upon you as it was upon Abraham, Jacob and Noah.

Noah Tithed

Yes, lest we forget, Noah was probably the first tither. In fact, he gave God more than a tenth. He gave God a seventh. One of every clean animal was sacrificed by Noah to the Lord when he came out of the Ark. *"And the Lord smelled a sweet savour; and the Lord said in his heart, I will not again curse the ground any more for man's sake; for the imagination of man's heart is evil from his youth; neither will I again smite any more every thing living, as I have done. While the earth remaineth, seedtime and harvest, and cold and heat, and summer and winter, and day and night shall not cease. And God blessed Noah..."* (Genesis 8:21,22; 9:1)

The Benefits Of Tithing And Giving To God

There are many benefits that come through tithing.
1. **God's promise of supplying all our needs:** Malachi 3:10, *"Bring ye all the tithes into the storehouse, that there may be meat in mine house, and prove me now herewith, saith the Lord of hosts, if I will not open you the windows of heaven, and pour you out a blessing, that there shall not be room enough to receive it."*

170

God has promised that He would pour out His blessing upon us so abundantly that our "storehouses" would be too small to receive it all. I believe that many people's needs are not met because they do not tithe and give to others. This is the reason many Americans are on welfare. If they would even begin to tithe out of their welfare cheques, God would begin to miraculously supply their needs, give them good jobs, and they would soon be able to get off the welfare programme.

2. **God will rebuke the devourer when we tithe.** (Malachi 3:11) Many things "devour" our possessions — storms, hail, fire, floods, pestilence, wars, and even grasshoppers. God has promised He would rebuke the devourer. This includes rust, mould, accidents, law-suits, and even flat tyres.

What "devours" your finances? Have you noticed that something is devouring your finances, such as unemployment, inefficient workmanship, incompetent mechanics or con-artists? God can protect you from these unscrupulous people. Your clothes will last longer, your tyres will drive longer, your vehicles and your machines won't break down every few days. The hands that pay their tithes are blessed hands.

3. **Your health shall spring forth speedily.** (Isaiah 58:7,8) This scripture clearly tells us that a fast to which God has called us is that of sharing our bread with the hungry, bringing the poor and those that are cast our to our house, clothing the naked and not turning away from the needs of our own family. He says that when we do these things, then our health shall spring forth speedily. We bring our bodies under God's divine protection, and the devourer cannot take away our health.

It seems that this verse not only promises a quick

171

return to good health when we care for others and give, but that it will cause us to live in a new dimension with God's light and glory breaking in upon our souls. I believe that God's good and generous givers have the glory of God upon their lives. There is a peculiar connection between giving, tithing and the glory of God.

We Dare Not Touch God's Portion

I believe that when God told Adam and Eve that they could eat from all the trees of the Garden, except the tree of the knowledge of good and evil, God was teaching them the law which He taught Israel — the devoted thing belongs to God, and it was to be given to the tribe of Levi, who ministered to God. *"Every thing devoted in Israel shall be thine."* (Numbers 18:14) *"...every devoted thing is most holy unto the Lord."* (Leviticus 27:28b)

So important was this law that when one man, Achan, from the tribe of Judah broke it, he brought a curse on Israel. God told Joshua, that they could not stand before their enemies because one man in the camp had stolen that which God had said must be brought into the treasury of the Lord. (Joshua 7:12) God said, *"And ye, in any wise keep yourselves from the accursed thing, lest ye make yourselves accursed, when ye take of the accursed thing, and make the camp of Israel a curse, and trouble it. But all the silver, and gold, and vessels of brass and iron, are consecrated unto the Lord: they shall come into the treasury of the Lord."* (Joshua 6:18,19)

God claimed the silver, gold, iron and brass for Himself. When Achan saw them in the ruins of Jericho, he coveted them and hid them in his tent. (Joshua 7:21)

Israel suffered great defeat at Ai and Achan caused the

172

death of 36 people besides his own and his family's, all because of his greed.

When we take the thing that is devoted to God, even the thing that belongs to Him, we cause a terrible curse to come upon us and our families, just like Achan did. God is a good and generous God, but He will not condone our stealing from Him.

Adam And Eve Lost The Glory Of God

When Adam and Eve ate from the tree of the knowledge of good and evil which God had told them they must never eat, (Genesis 2:17) they lost the glory of God. God said they could eat from all the trees of the garden, but one, that one, was "the devoted tree." It was God's tree. When they ate from it, they committed the same sin as Achan did. The glory of God lifted from them. They found themselves naked. They were not able to possess the blessings which God had already given to them.

Why America Is Blessed

God has blessed America. As long as we tithe and give to our needy neighbours and even to our enemies, for Jesus told us to do it, God will continue to bless America. Jesus said, *"Love your enemies, bless them that curse you, do good to them that hate you, and pray for them which despitefully use you, and persecute you; That ye may be the children of your Father which is in heaven...."* (Matthew 5:44,45) That means that we should even bless the Communist nations that hate us. I believe that we have done this, and God has blessed us for it, though many cannot understand this high law of love. But when we stop

173

giving to others, so we can pay our own national debt, the bottom will drop out and we will become a bankrupt nation over night. Watch the nations who are in economic crisis. They are the ones that have not given to others. They dammed up the flow of God's supply. Holding back from giving dams up the flow of God's river of blessing from His treasure house.

Give Generously

Never give in a skimpy way or begrudgingly. Never pretend to give more than you give. Ananias and Sapphira claimed they gave God everything, when in secret they had held back a portion for themselves. This grieved the Holy Ghost and He became their enemy.

When Mary poured out the ointment on Jesus, she poured it all out, for she broke the alabaster box. It is impossible to keep anything back when you break up that which contains the precious treasure. That's why God allows our hearts to be broken, so He can have our all.

Give to God without reservation, and it shall be given to you — *"good measure, pressed down, and shaken together, and running over, shall men give into your bosom. For with the same measure that ye mete withal it shall be measured to you again."* (Luke 6:38)

Remember, God said, *"...He which soweth sparingly shall reap also sparingly; and he which soweth bountifully shall reap also bountifully. Every man according as he purposeth in his heart, so let him give; not grudgingly, or of necessity: for God loveth a cheerful giver. And God is able to make all grace abound toward you; that ye, always having all sufficiency in all things, may abound to every good work."* (II Corinthians 9:6,7,8)

In this same chapter there is a tremendous verse. It is the tenth verse, *"Now he that ministereth seed to the sower both minister bread for your food, and multiply your seed sown, and increase the fruits of your righteousness."* In this verse God has promised that if we give, we will suffer no lack. If you sow, He will give you seed which you can sow. He will give you bread to eat. It was the duty of Boaz to set bread before the field workers. He even reached his parched corn to Ruth and she did eat. (Ruth 2:14)

As you sow (by giving to others), God will give you more seed to sow. He will give you your food and He will multiply the seed you have sown that it may bring forth righteous seed on your behalf. You may never be able to go to a mission field to save souls, but when you give to send and support others, God will bless your sacrifice by giving you fruits of righteousness.

The Curse

It is very important that we know that there is a curse that comes upon us when we rob God of His tithes and offerings. Malachi 3:8 says, *"Will a man rob God? Yet ye have robbed me. But ye say, Wherein have we robbed thee? In tithes and offerings."*

When we rob God, we bring great trouble upon ouselves just like Adam and Eve, Achan, and Ananias and Sapphira (Acts 5:1-11) did.

God says, *"Ye are cursed with a curse: for ye have robbed me, even this whole nation."* (Malachi 3:9) The whole nation was cursed because the whole nation robbed God.

I cannot warn you too strongly. I have seen too many lives destroyed because of lack of knowledge. God says,

"My people are destroyed for lack of knowledge...." (Hosea 4:6)

Who Should Tithe?

Everyone! God will even bless the sinner who tithes, for he has entered into the law of sowing and reaping.

The children should be taught to tithe when they are given their first allowance. It should become a part of their lives.

The old should know that even living on a limited income does not exclude them from daring to trust God, and giving Him their tenth. He can heal them so they don't need medicine. People will love them and care for them. I believe many who end up in "rest homes" or nursing homes, forgotten by all, waiting to die, are those who never were tithers. King David said, *"I have been young, and now am old; yet have I not seen the righteous forsaken, nor his seed begging bread."* (Psalm 37:25)

Those on welfare should tithe. To those who are on social security, welfare, pensions and similar means of monthly support I would like to say, you need to be faithful with your tithes, lest God allow your income to be cut off. You live off the mercy of others which is very insecure. But if you give to God, you live off the mercy of God, and He can cause others to be merciful to you.

Churches should tithe. I know this may surprise you, but I firmly believe that every church should give one tenth of its income to missionary ministries and to other ministries as well. God will bless the missionary church in a miraculous way. I would not belong to a church that had no missionary vision and which did not give at least one tenth of its income (before the bills are paid) to the mission field.

176

If the churches had tithed to missions, I believe the Gospel would have gone throughout all the earth long ago.

Ministries should tithe to other ministries. Maybe you do not have a church, but you have a ministry. You should also tithe from your ministry to other ministries. God will richly bless you for giving to other ministries and you shall have no lack.

How Much Is A Tithe?

A tithe is ten percent of all that you earn **before** deductions are made from your salary and **before** your bills are paid. Be generous with God, and He will be generous with you.

What About Offerings?

Offerings are over and above our tithes. Remember, Israel gave in three ways:

1. their firstfruits,
2. their tenth,
3. their offerings.

As long as Israel gave, they were blessed.

God warned us that if we keep everything we make or earn, we will lose it. He said, *"...Consider your ways. Ye have sown much, and bring in little; ye eat, but ye have not enough; ye drink, but ye are not filled with drink; ye clothe you, but there is none warm; and he that earneth wages earneth wages to put it into a bag with holes."* (Haggai 1:5,6)

God then says, "Build My house first, and then your own."

"But seek ye first the kingdom of God, and his righteousness; and all these things shall be added unto you." (Matthew 6:33) Most of us seek the "added" things. If we seek God's Kingdom first, we will never have to seek for the added things or the temporal things.

Where Should You Tithe?

This is a very controversial subject. The Word of God says, "Bring it into the storehouse." The storehouse is the place where you get your meat, bread and wine. Where do you get your spiritual food? Give to that cause!

Jesus told us to multiply our talents. Does the ministry to which you give bear fruit? Are souls being saved? If not, give where you know you will have righteous seed, for God commanded us to be fruitful and multiply.

What does your church teach and believe? Does your church believe in salvation through grace, the blood of Jesus, the Baptism of the Holy Spirit with speaking in tongues and the other gifts of the Holy Spirit? Does it have a deliverance ministry? Or does it mock these things?

Paul said, *"I have not shunned to declare unto you all the counsel of God."* (Acts 20:27) Paul preached the whole Gospel, and we, too, must stand behind those who preach the whole Gospel. I am sure that Paul would have supported only those who preached the whole Gospel. I wouldn't support anything that didn't preach the full Gospel in word and in deed. It is not enough to say that we believe the full Gospel when we don't have the works thereof and the signs following.

Don't give to churches that support revolutionary and guerrilla armies whose terrorists kill the missionaries and the national preachers of the Gospel. A claim has been made that the World Council of Churches supports revolutions in Third World countries. Be careful not to buy bullets to kill Christians. Does your church belong to the World Council of Churches?

My Husband Won't Let Me Give

This is the lamest excuse I have ever heard. Women who use this excuse had better ask God what to do. Abigail's husband refused to give to David, so when he was "on a drunk" (I Samuel 25:36), she loaded up the asses with loaves of bread, bottles of wine, five sheep that were dressed, parched corn, clusters of raisins, cakes of figs, etc. and made a secret donation to the Lord's anointed which saved many lives.

Many women hide behind their husbands when they themselves are more stingy about giving than their husbands.

Our Chinese women took their tithes out of their grocery money every week and brought it to the house of the Lord on Sunday with much joy.

A woman I knew whose husband forbade her to give money to the Lord, supported a missionary couple who were preparing for the mission field in language school by saving up some of her grocery every week and delivering these boxes of groceries to them. It was a great blessing to them and they practically lived from the grocery they received from this woman.

You can always buy Christian books from ministries. Perhaps your husband wouldn't mind you spending your money on something he can see, such as buying books or other things that are for sale. I know of some that do this.

Give clothes. You can always give some of your clothing to missionaries and to others in the Lord's work

179

who have need of it. If half your dresses were missing, your husband wouldn't even know the difference. You don't really need much of the things that you have in your house. You can also give jewelry as unto the Lord. There are many ways of giving into the Lord's work.

You can get a job and earn your own money. Never use your husband as an excuse. You cannot fool God. You have talents. Use them for God. Ask God. He will show you how to give.

I have known women who blamed their lack of giving on their husbands, but when their husbands died and they had it in their hands to give, they were no better than he had been. Where there is a heart to give, a way will be found.

Conclusion

There are many more things that can be said about giving and many scriptures that will prove our point, but this is not a book on tithing. It is a study on how to win the battle over the enemy through the means of God's end-time battle-plan. I want you to win every battle and so does God. That is why I draw your attention to this important truth of giving. If you cheat God, there is a weakness in your ranks. You cannot stand before your enemy. Pay your tithes. Touch not the devoted thing and God will reward you and bless you, and you will win a glorious victory over your enemy on every front.

STUDY QUESTIONS

1. Read Genesis 14, Genesis 28:22-30:43, Hebrews 7:1-10.

2. Memorize Malachi 3:10.

3. What is the key to God's provision?

4. How much are we to give to God?

5. Should only those who have a permanent job tithe?

CONCLUSION

I have come to the conclusion of this Bible study on God's end-time plan for warfare.

I know there are other "weapons" such as fasting, intercessory prayer and the power of the precious Blood of Jesus. I have already written complete Bible studies that deal with these powerful weapons.

The foregoing are the ones that God particularly laid upon my heart to bring before His people. This is a subject that has been on my heart since I wrote the Bible study on intercessory prayer, *Pour Out Your Heart* seven years ago. Because of my busy life in the ministry, it has not been possible for me to prepare this study earlier. I pray that it will be a blessing to you and help you in your spiritual warfare. Things will not get easier. Satan has come down, knowing his time is short. The battle will get harder, but we are not helpless. God has made us strong and He has fully equipped us for that which faces us in the future. I believe that through Jesus Christ we are more than conquerors.

Let us go on to total victory through Christ Jesus, our Lord.

CLASSIC ANOINTED BIBLE STUDIES

BEHOLD THE BRIDEGROOM COMETH!— *Gwen Shaw*. A Bible study on the soon return of Jesus Christ. With so many false teachings these days, it is important that we realize how imminent the rapture of the saints of God really is ....#100-37 $6.50

ENDUED WITH LIGHT TO REIGN FOREVER — *Gwen Shaw*. This deeply profound Bible study reveals the characteristics of the eternal, supernatural, creative light of God as found in His Word. The "Father of Lights," created man in His image. He longs for man to step out of darkness and into His light ....#101-71 $6.00

GOD'S END-TIME BATTLE-PLAN—*Gwen Shaw*. This study on spiritual warfare gives you the biblical weapons for spiritual warfare such as victory through dancing, shouting, praising, uplifted hands, marching, etc. It has been a great help to many who have been bound by tradition ....#102-35 $8.00

IT'S TIME FOR REVIVAL—*Gwen Shaw*. A Bible Study on Revival that not only gives scriptural promises of the end-time Revival, but also presents the stories of revivals in the past and the revivalists whom God used. It will stir your heart and encourage you to believe for great revival .....#103-24 $7.75

OUR MINISTERING ANGELS—*Gwen Shaw*. A scriptural Bible study on the topic of angels. Angels will be playing a more and more prominent part in these last days. We need to understand about them and their ministry ....#104-87 $7.50

POUR OUT YOUR HEART—*Gwen Shaw*. A wonderful Bible study on travailing prayer. The hour has come to intercede before the throne of God. The call to intercession is for everyone, and we must carry the Lord's burden and weep for the lost so that the harvest can be brought in quickly ....#105-16 $5.00

REDEEMING THE LAND—*Gwen Shaw*. This important teaching will help you know your authority through the Blood of Jesus to dislodge evil spirits, break the curse, and restore God's blessing upon the land. A Bible study on spiritual warfare..#108-61 $9.50

THE FINE LINE—*Gwen Shaw*. This Bible study clearly magnifies the "fine line" difference between the soul realm and the spirit realm. Both are intangible and therefore cannot be discerned with the five senses, but must be discerned by the Holy Spirit and the Word of God. A must for the deeper Christian..#101-91 $6.00

THE POWER OF THE PRECIOUS BLOOD—*Gwen Shaw*. A Bible study on the Blood of Jesus. The author shares how it was revealed to her how much Satan fears Jesus' Blood. This Bible study will help you overcome and destroy the works of Satan in your life and the lives of loved ones ....#105-18 $5.00

THE POWER OF PRAISE—*Gwen Shaw*. When God created the heavens and earth He was surrounded by praise. Miracles happen when holy people praise a Holy God! Praise is the language of creation. If prayer can move the hand of God, how much more praise can move Him! ....#400-66 $5.00

YE SHALL RECEIVE POWER FROM ON HIGH *Gwen Shaw.* This is a much needed foundational teaching on the Baptism of the Holy Spirit. It will enable you to teach this subject, as well as to understand these truths more fully yourself..#107-37 $5.00

YOUR APPOINTMENT WITH GOD—*Gwen Shaw.* A Bible study on fasting. Fasting is one of the most neglected sources of power over bondages of Satan that God has given the Church. The author's experiences are shared in this Bible study in a way that will change your life ....#107-40 $5.00

IN-DEPTH BIBLE STUDIES

FORGIVE AND RECEIVE—An In-Depth Bible Study on Philemon for the Serious Student of God's Word—*Gwen Shaw.* This Bible Study is a lesson to the church on the much-needed truths of forgiveness and restoration. The epistle to Philemon came from the heart of Paul who had experienced great forgiveness ....#102-01 $7.00

GRACE ALONE—An In-Depth Bible Study on Galatians for the Serious Student of God's Word—*Gwen Shaw.* This study teaches the reader to gain freedom in the finished work of the Cross by forsaking works which cannot add to salvation and live by *Grace Alone* ....#108-47 $13.00

MYSTERY REVEALED—An In-Depth Bible Study on Ephesians for the Serious Student of God's Word—*Gwen Shaw.* Search the depths of God's riches in one of Paul's most profound epistles, "to the praise of His glory!" Learn the "mystery" of the united Body of Christ.......#104-53 $15.00

OUR GLORIOUS HEAD—An In-Depth Bible Study on Colossians for the Serious Student of God's Word—*Gwen Shaw.* This book teaches vital truths for today, assisting the reader in discerning false teachings, when the philosophies of men are being promoted as being the truths of God. Jesus Christ is the Head of His Body ....#104-85 $9.00

THE CATCHING AWAY!—An In-Depth Bible Study on First and Second Thessalonians —*Gwen Shaw.* This is a very timely Bible Study because Jesus is coming soon! The book of I Thessalonians explains God's revelation to Paul on the rapture of the saints. II Thessalonians reveals what will happen after the rapture when the antichrist takes over ....#100-88 $13.00

THE LOVE LETTER—An In-Depth Bible Study on Philippians for the Serious Student of God's Word—*Gwen Shaw.* Another of Gwen Shaw's expository Bibles Studies on the books of the Bible. This study of the letter to the first church of Europe will give the reader an understanding of Paul's great love for the church that was born out of his suffering.........#103-99 $9.00

BIBLE COURSE

THE TRIBES OF ISRAEL—*Gwen Shaw.* This popular and well-loved study on the thirteen tribes of Israel will show you your place in the spiritual tribes in these last days. Better understand yourself and others through the study of this Bible Course ....#106-70 $45.00

OTHER BOOKS BY GWEN SHAW

LOVE, THE LAW OF THE ANGELS—*Gwen Shaw*. This is undoubtedly the greatest of Gwen Shaw's writings. It carries a message of healing and life in a sad and fallen civilization. Love heals the broken-hearted and sets disarray in order. You will never be the same after reading this beautiful book about love. (Also available in French) ....Paperback #103-97 $10.00

SONG OF LOVE—*Gwen Shaw*. She was a heart-broken missionary, far from home. She cried out to God for help. He spoke, "Turn to the Song of Solomon and read!" As she turned in obedience, the Lord took her into the "Throne Room" of Heaven and taught her about the love of Christ for His Bride, the church. She fell in love with Jesus afresh, and you will too ....#108-62 $7.50

THE FALSE FAST — *Gwen Shaw*. Now, from the pen of Gwen Shaw, author of *Your Appointment With God* (a Bible Study on fasting), comes an exposé on the False Fast. It will help you to examine your motives for fasting, and make your foundations sure, so that your fast will be a potent tool in the hands of God 115-62 $2.50

THE LIGHT WILL COME FROM RUSSIA — *Gwen Shaw*. The thrilling testimony of Mother Barbara, Abbess of the Mount of Olives in Jerusalem. She shares prophecies which were given to her concerning the nations of the world in our time by a holy bishop of the Kremlin, ten days before his death just prior to the Russian Revolution ....#116-24 $3.95

TO BE LIKE JESUS — *Gwen Shaw*. Based on her Throne Room experience in 1971, the author shares the Father's heart about our place as sons in His Family. Nothing is more important than *To Be Like Jesus*! ....#116-51 $6.95

THE PARABLE OF THE GOLDEN RAIN—*Gwen Shaw*. This is the story of how revivals come and go, and a true picture, in parable language, of how the Church tries to replace the genuine move of the Spirit with man-made programs and tactics. It's amusing and convicting at the same time...............#104-94 $4.00

THEY SHALL MOUNT UP WITH WINGS AS EAGLES—*Gwen Shaw*. Though you may feel old or tired, if you wait on the Lord, you shall mount up on wings as eagles! Let this book encourage you to stretch your wings and fulfill your destiny—no matter what your age! ....#116-22 $6.95

Prices are subject to change.

For a complete listing of Engeltal Press books, please write or call:

Engeltal Press
P.O. Box 447
Jasper, AR 72641
Tel. (870) 446-2665 • Fax (870) 446-2259
www.engeltalpress.com

Ad 4